FATHER'S MEMORABLE JOKES

A DAD AND HIS JOKES

ALFIE THOMAS

Book title Copyright © 2022 by Alfie Thomas. All rights reserved. Printed in the United States of America. No part of this book may be used or reproduced in any manner whatsoever without written permission except in the case of brief quotations.

Copyright © 2022 by Alfie Thomas

All rights reserved. No part of this publication may be reproduced, distributed or transmitted in any form or by any means, including photocopying, recording or any other electronic or mechanical methods, without the prior written permission of the publisher, except in the case of brief quotations embodied in critical reviews and certain other noncommercial uses permitted by copyright law.

Although the publisher and the author have made every effort to ensure that the information in this book was correct at press time and while this publication is designed to provide accurate information in regard to the subject matter overall, the publisher and author assume no responsibility for errors, inaccuracies, omissions or any other inconsistences herein and hereby disclaim any liability to any party for any loss, damage or disruption caused by errors or omission, whether such errors or omissions result from negligence, accident or any other cause.

This publication is meant as a source of valuable information for the reader, however, it's not meant as a substitute for direct expertise assistance. If such level of assistance is required, the services of a competent professional should be sought.

CONTENTS

Are You Trying to be Funny?   7

1. THE IMPORTANCE OF HUMOR   17
   What is Humor?   17
   The Importance of Humor   18
   Can Humor be Taught?   20
2. WARM UP THE YOUNGSTERS WITH A ONE-LINER   23
3. ANIMAL ANTICS   31
4. MAKING FUN OF THE FAMILY   41
5. FOOD FOR THOUGHT   53
6. WHOLE BODY GIGGLES   63
7. CRACKS ABOUT POP CULTURE   73
8. JESTING ABOUT JOBS   83
9. HORSING AROUND WITH HOBBIES   91
10. THE ESCAPADES OF EDUCATION   101
11. WISECRACKS FOR THE ROAD   113
12. STEM   123
13. POP'S PUNS FOR THE TEENS   137
    Engaging Teens With Humor   146
14. MORE THAN A ONE-LINER   149
15. THE BEST OF THE BEST   193

That's a Wrap, Folks!   201
References   209

For Mercy, Ava, and Mia

"I keep all my Dad Jokes in a Dad-a-Base"

— UNKNOWN

ARE YOU TRYING TO BE FUNNY?

I was a quiet and shy 12 year old who liked to keep to myself. I was usually reading, playing outside, or spending time with my best friend. One day at school, I got into a verbal argument with an older student during recess. I was pretty upset and angry about it, and by the time I got home, my mood had not improved. It was middle school. I was a pre-teen; hence, I was already going through enough in life. When my father returned from work, he picked up on my low energy and mood. He asked me what the matter was, and when the response he received was silence, he said, "what did one wig say to another wig?"

Even though I was initially reluctant to respond, I said, "I don't know."

He responded, "Can you hair me?"

I couldn't help but laugh. That was all it took for me to feel better—a sweet dad joke. It was thoughtful and well-timed, and once I eased up, he asked what the matter was. Surprisingly, it felt easier relating the story to him.

My father was and still is the king of dad jokes. Every time I hear a dad joke, I remember my father because I associate humor with him. If you don't know what dad jokes are, then you're not from this planet. The definition even exists in the dictionary, "a wholesome joke of the type said to be told by fathers with a punch line that is often an obvious or predictable pun or play on words and usually judged to be endearingly corny or unfunny" (*Definition of a Dad Joke*, n.d.).

You would think because they are jokes, they are funny, but don't be fooled my friend. They are not always funny; they typically garner the following response, "Oh my God Dad, you are not funny" or "Dad, that's lame." Depending on the mood and age of my children, I have also earned a loud laugh or giggling. So, why do we even tell dad jokes if that's the response? Well, I do it to amuse my daughters and get a reaction from them. It's a shared bond and sense of humor amongst us. I know when they are feeling low or in a bad mood, all I must do is crack a dad joke, and the mood lightens.

However, I am in no way using humor as a tool to deflect from their feelings. We do talk about their feelings when they want to. There are days when the younger two curl up in my lap and say, "Daddy, make me laugh," and honestly it's one of the sweetest moments.

My daughters (Alfie's angels—Mercy, Ava and Mia) must know all my jokes by now. They are 10 and under, and it's that adorable age where I can get laughs in return for my dad jokes. So, you can gauge how many jokes I must have in my arsenal by now.

However, I am not the only one cracking dad jokes in my family—it actually dates back to my father—the original dad joker! As far as I can recall, a day did not go by when my father wouldn't crack a dad joke. Even now, every phone conversation ends with one and my response of, "Ha-ha, dad. I love you, bye." Naturally, when my angels were born, I couldn't wait to start joking with them. I waited until they were old enough to comprehend what a joke is, and then the onslaught began. My father helps to carry on this tradition with my daughters; hence, every time he meets them, he makes sure to crack a joke or two with them. These moments are heartwarming and make me smile. The girls also look forward to listening to their grandfather's jokes, so he still has that amazing sense of humor.

Jokes aside, making your children laugh, getting a funny reaction from them, and being able to lighten their mood is a beautiful feeling for a father. It makes me feel closer to my daughters, and it strengthens our bond. As Milton Berle said, "Laughter is the best medicine in the world."

I want to showcase the importance of laughter, joy, and familial bonds for getting us through the ups and downs of life and the benefits of being there for your family. Through my emphasis on these matters, I want to tell you how you can recreate the same dynamics with your children. Moreover, psychological research indicates that humor increases intimacy and reduces stress (Mitchell, 2019).

Furthermore, studies have proven the following benefits and impacts on children when humor is present within a family (*Why Being Funny Is Good for Your Family | Parenting Tips & Advice*, n.d.):

- Children with a developed sense of humor are more intelligent and creative.
- Humor encourages comprehension skills.
- Humor helps children learn and retain lessons much better.
- Humor can decrease stress and enable easier social interactions.

Who knew jokes could be so beneficial?

I want to clarify that any joke doesn't work on any age group, especially if it's your children in question. You have to know your audience. The following is a timeline for you to understand what kind of humor you can employ at which age.

FROM BIRTH ONWARD: SLAPSTICK

Untill your child turns two, the only humor they will understand is physical and action-oriented humor. It will be silly and ridiculous, but it's what it's. Walk around like a penguin, make silly faces, do funny dances, and so on.

Children, surprisingly enough, are responsive to physical comedy and humor from an early age. Even five-month-old babies find silly and ridiculous movements funny. Did you know that by the time they turn eight-months-old, babies begin to make their own jokes, even though they don't have the ability to talk? They do this through actions, such as making silly faces and noises.

If you are wondering why children this age find slapstick humor funny and not scary, it's because you have a big smile on your face while performing these actions. Children are intuitive and can read emotions such as happiness, sadness, and anger easily. Experiment to see what makes your child laugh and build around those actions.

TWO AND ABOVE: "LYING" ABOUT

As your child nears the two-year-old mark, you will notice that they have developed verbal and language skills. Even if they are not conversing, they can comprehend all that you are conveying to them. Hence, verbal jokes can have the desired effect on them—a lot of laughter.

Why I refer to this age group as "lying" about is because lies (harmless lies and funny lies, not life changing lies please) are easy for the children to comprehend—lies that everyone knows are definitely not true. For instance:

- Isn't the grass a beautiful shade of blue today?
- Come for lunch, we are having a wooly mammoth.
- If you aren't in the mood to go to school, I can go in your place and play with your friends.

The ridiculousness is what will make them laugh.

THREE AND ABOVE: LET'S RHYME

By this age, children begin to develop phonological awareness. What is phonological awareness? It's the child's ability to understand and recognize the words, rhymes, syllables, and segments of a sentence. Due to this new development and attentiveness, children begin to learn that words rhyme, and replacing a word with a rhyme is funny to them.

For instance, "Can you please pass me the salt and *letter?*" instead of salt and *pepper*.

Even Knock Knock jokes can help warm your child up to understand and recognize what actual jokes are. You can start with the most basic of jokes.

"Knock knock."

"Who's there?"

"Boo."

"Boo who?"

"Stop crying and let me in!"

FOUR AND ABOVE: WORD PLAY

When your child's language skills begin to further develop, they start to appreciate well worded jokes.

Synonyms, homonyms, nuanced words, rhymes, and multiple meaning words become recognizable. For instance: "Which fish will cost you a lot? A goldfish."

So go ahead, have fun with your children and make each other laugh.

When Mirabelle and I got divorced, it was a tough time for our daughters and us. It's a challenging time when emotions are stretched, and there are geographical and emotional changes. My daughters were extremely upset, as was I. Our family structure had changed, and it was difficult for them to come to terms with it. For this reason, I tried my best to give my daughters one small familiarity as a sense of comfort—my dad jokes. I hope that it helped them in some way.

I want to be able to spread the same joy and love that my father did by passing along his jokes. He doesn't know this, but ever since I heard his first dad joke, I began to keep a journal of all the dad jokes he makes. It has been over 30 years now, and my father is still at it, and I am still busy filling in those journals. I now have around 30 journals filled with his jokes! I am sitting on a treasure. (Sshh…don't tell him!)

This book is not just for fathers, it's for grandfathers, uncles, soon to be fathers, sons, and anyone who has a sense of humor and likes to entertain others. Just to clarify, this isn't gender specific either. Even mothers, daughters, aunts, and nieces can enjoy this book or gift it forward. Sometimes we get so caught up with our daily lives, that we forget how important it's to step back, breathe, smile, and laugh. This book will help you do just that.

It's possible that you feel distant from your children and want to use humor to forge a stronger connection. Maybe you want to be the fun parent and put a smile on their face or a laugh in their hearts by telling jokes. Perhaps you just need to brush up on your dad joke repertoire. If any of these are true for you, this book is can help you.

I will provide you with a vast selection of dad jokes, from the classics to the latest, categorized in different themes. The jokes range from ridiculously corny to witty and intelligent for any audience, whether that's your 3-year-old child or your 80-year-old-granny. Moreover, this book has:

- an extensive list of one-liners and puns that will make any audience laugh
- the ability to bring a crowd of people or a family together with some humor
- new lines for when the knock-knock and pirate jokes are too outdated for your children

- the chances to create bonds—with your children or your parents
- the health benefits of laughing, such as reduced stress and more oxygen in the brain

It is not only us every day dads cracking dad jokes, but celebrities are also on the same bandwagon as well. Take Conan O'Brien, for instance. He tweeted, "I just taught my kids about taxes by eating 38% of their ice-cream." I don't know how that must have landed with his children, considering he ate their ice-cream, but celebrity fathers are in the same boat as us!

So, I want to share snippets of laughter, giggles, eye rolls, and fun to further share with your family and friends. There were days when I was down while compiling this book, but believe me when I say writing and compiling the jokes had me smiling and laughing in no time. I hope this book can offer the same for you. Get ready to enjoy yourself on this funny ride with me! I hope you can keep your laughter contained—no promises on that front.

Let's get started!

1

THE IMPORTANCE OF HUMOR

WHAT IS HUMOR?

Honestly, the best way to ruin a joke is to go into detail and explain it, but right now, I am going to do that and explain to you what psychologists believe about humor. There are three main theories on humor and where it originates. The three main theories are:

- relief theory
- superiority theory
- incongruity theory

The relief theory states that humor and laughter are defense mechanisms and ways of channeling stress and anxiety. In a way, it releases the nervous and stressful energy. As evidence of this theory, notice that jokes cracked at funerals are not met with silence, instead they are met with laughter.

The superiority theory originates from Aristotle and Plato. They sought to make us understand a specific type of humor—laughing at other people's misfortunes and unfortunate circumstances. This theory suggests that when humor is employed in such instances, it's declaring one's superiority over the other individual. If you are looking to break the ice or build relationships, this is not the type of humor you should be employing.

The incongruity theory states that humor is the result of two different and contrasting ideas mingling. Humor undermines the general expectation, and punch lines are the outcomes of an unforeseen reversal.

Ask yourself which type of humor you employ the most.

THE IMPORTANCE OF HUMOR

We think comedy and jokes are just about a relaxing laugh, but laughter is extremely important to the mental well-being and flourishing of the human mind. Mark Twain said it best when he said, "Humanity has unquestionably one really effective weapon, laughter."

Laughter has the ability to impact our health. It's the best stress reliever. A good bout of laughter can keep the muscles in our entire body relaxed for up to 45 minutes. Imagine cracking a few good jokes all day long, you will never have a crick in your neck or a backache, and this is something I can help you with along the course of the book! I promise that.

Dr. Gulshan Sethi, a cardio surgeon in Tucson medical Centre says laughter is like internal jogging, it tones all the internal organs and strengthens the abdomen without doing a single sit-up. Time to say goodbye to exercise and imagine replacing 30 minutes on the treadmill with 30 minutes of non-stop laughter! What would you prefer?

Laughter induces better social relations. The contagious nature of a smile or a good laugh helps us to connect with others, leading to friendships and even romantic closeness. In fact couples who laugh together are more likely to stay married longer. People who have enduring friendships are also proven to outlive those who have fewer friends.

Laughter boosts our body's immune response. Studies have found that laughing in a funny movie or finding humor in a stressful situation helps to increase the production of natural killer cells—white blood cells that attack cancer, colds, and foreign bacteria. Laughter combats depression. When we laugh our body dumps a bunch of good neurons peptides into our blood stream including oxytocin and dopamine.

Laughter reduces physical pain. Perceived pain levels in participants of many different studies are lowered when they laugh. Laughter is a measurable trait found to be higher in those who are more resilient. If you find a successful person who can take the punches of life just as easily as the accolades, you will find someone who laughs a lot.

We know by instinct that humor is important in relationships. The reasons are often left vague. It's not that we only crudely want entertainment; we don't want to just laugh per se. For two people to be able to tolerate one another over time, they will need to be able to laugh in the nicest way at each other and at themselves. This goes for every relation in our lives.

CAN HUMOR BE TAUGHT?

Are we just born funny, or can we become funny overtime? Everyone has that one friend who is naturally funny. I am that one friend in my social circle. Maybe I got it from my father! Who knows? The positives of humor are so great that Stanford University is offering business courses on humor in the workplace.

You may find yourself asking why? Well, they want to teach students effective and creative ways of running organizations, building social bonds with ease, and making good memories. Sounds great, doesn't it? Moreover, the professors of this course are of the belief that humor is a powerful tool which can be employed to bring about positive changes. I for one would love to work with a funny and easy-going boss as opposed to a serious boss.

Coming back to the original point, is humor inherent or learned? Let me put your mind at ease, every human has an inborn sense of humor, but the tricky part is that everyone will not have a good sense of humor. Yes, good is subjective, but by good I mean a humor that appeals to the majority of others. Being informed about the theories of humor, researching it, and learning punch lines will not make you funnier. There is more to it—genetics. Sorry folks, if you have serious parents and grandparents, you might not be able to develop a good sense of humor. Researchers have connected humor to a variant of the 5-HTTLPR gene which indicates humor.

However, most psychologists are still debating over whether humor is inborn or learned. You see, nobody is not funny, most people just suppress humor and don't allow themselves the leeway of easing up. Laughter and humor is an integral part of human nature. You can still read up on jokes, punch lines, look on the funny and brighter side of things, laugh at silly things, and so on! You don't have to be cracking jokes 24/7 to be the funniest person. Sometimes humor is found in the most unexpected places and spaces.

In the next chapter I am going to reveal a treasure trove of jokes covering family friendly and children friendly dad jokes. Read on to see what I have in store for you.

Time to get funny!

2

WARM UP THE YOUNGSTERS WITH A ONE-LINER

Let's begin, shall we? Are you ready to laugh, roll your eyes, or snicker? Before I begin, I want to clarify that I don't tell dad jokes to just my children, I tell dad jokes every chance I get, and I want the same for you. If you find a good opportunity and the timing is right, go for it, let out that funny side of yours.

I will start with jokes that young children will also be able to appreciate, which they can then further share with whoever they want. However, a little warning: children are unpredictable when it comes to dad jokes. You never know what their reaction may be. Will you be met with a blank stare, a horrified expression, a loud laugh, a small giggle, or a groan? Whatever it may be, have faith in your skills, the reaction will always be entertaining if nothing else.

The top 50 children friendly dad jokes are:

1. Why did the math problem look so sad?
Because of all its problems

2. What did the police officer say to the belly button?
You're under a vest.

3. Why did the coffee go to the police?
It got mugged.

4. What did the slow tomato say to the others?
Don't worry; I will ketchup.

5. How does Darth Vader like his toast?
On the dark side

6. Why did the coach go to the bank?
To get his quarter back

7. How do celebrities stay cool?
They have lots of fans.

8. Why do melons have weddings?
Because they cantaloupe

9. What did the fisherman say to the magician?
Pick a cod, any cod.

10. What do you call a fake noodle?
An impasta

11. Why don't eggs tell jokes?
They'd crack each other up.

12. Did you hear the rumor about butter?
Better not spread it.

13. Why don't crabs give to charity?
Because they're shellfish

14. What did one ocean say to the other?
Nothing, they just waved.

15. What kind of cheese can never be yours?
Nacho cheese

16. What will you call the bears without ears?
B!

17. Does anyone over here need an ark?
I Noah Guy!

18. When does a tailor go on a vacation?
When they seam stressed

19. What's the best joke about construction?
I'm still working on it!

20. Why did the banana go to the hospital?
He was peeling really bad.

21. What do you call a nosy pepper?
Jalapeno business

22. Why did the kid throw a stick of butter out the window?
To see butter-fly

23. Why do you smear peanut butter in the road?
To go with the traffic jam

24. What do you call an attractive fruit?
A fine-apple

25. What did the cupcake tell its frosting?
I would be muffin without you.

26. Why did the witches' team lose the baseball game?
Their bats flew away.

27. What starts with E, ends with E, and has only 1 letter in it?
Envelope

28. Why shouldn't you give Elsa a balloon?
Because she will let it go

29. Why does your nose run?
Because it can't walk

30. What do you call the child of parents from Iceland and Cuba?
An ice cube

31. Have you heard how popular the local cemetery is?
People are just dying to get in.

32. Why do skeletons stay so calm?
Because nothing gets under their skin

33. Dad to kid (in a serious voice): "A word of advice, kid. Never trust atoms. They make up everything."

34. Dad: "I never thought I'd be the type to have a beard, but then it just grew on me."

35. Dad to kids at dinner: "I would tell you my pizza joke, but it's just too cheesy."

36. Dad: "This book about how Newton discovered gravity is so good! I just can't put it down."

37. Want to hear a long joke?
Joooooooooooooooke

38. Kid: "Dad, it hurts when I move my arm like this."
Dad: "Then, don't move your arm like that."

39. Sore throats are a pain in the neck.

40. What do you call a belt made of watches?
A waist of time

41. What do you say when you lose a Wii game?
I want a wii-match.

42. Why did the balloon go near the needle?
He wanted to be a pop star.

43. What did the French boy do when he drank too much water?
He went *oui oui* in his pants.

44. Where do pencils spend their vacations?
In pencil-vania

45. What is invisible and smells of worms?
A bird's fart

46. How did one penny propose to the other penny?
He said, "together we make cents."

47. I slept like a log last night! I woke up in the fireplace.

48. What state has the smallest drinks?
Mini-soda

49. Why did the smart phone need glasses?
He lost his contacts.

50. What is the best day to cook?
Fry day

One day I picked Mercy up from soccer practice, and when she sat in the car, she had a sullen face. I asked her what was with the long face, and she mumbled something incoherently in return. I kept driving quietly while she was staring out the window. I put on her favorite song, waited for a minute more, and then said to her, "Mercy, I have a question for you." Her response was just a sidelong glance. "Why do you think Cinderella was bad at soccer?" Again, I was met with silence and sullen face. "Well, it was obviously because she was always running away from the ball." With that, she just smiled, a very small smile, shook her head in disbelief as if to say, "come on dad!" I told her we could talk about why she was upset if she wanted, and she just nodded and said, "okay," slightly less sullen. It did lighten her mood, just like my father had once done the same for me. It also manages to create memories, and honestly, I feel good when I can make my child smile after she has had a tough day.

I hope you are able to do the same in a similar situation.

In the next chapter I will share jokes on animals.

3

ANIMAL ANTICS

Who doesn't love animals? If you are an animal lover, you will love this section on animal dad jokes. As Anatole France once said, "Until one has loved an animal, a part of one's soul remains unawakened." Hence, I hope to spark the love of animals within you by sharing my animal dad jokes.

We are an animal loving family; we have a golden retriever named Fluffy (my daughters named him), and he is a part of the family.

Animal jokes are often the safest because they are enjoyed by all. We have all heard the one about the fish with no eye! If not, then read on. Nevertheless, there are far more original fish jokes and tons of dad jokes about animals and their antics that will "quack" you up.

The top 50 animal dad jokes are:

1. Why did the fish blush?
Because it saw the ocean's bottom

2. Boy: "Dad, can you put the cat out?
Dad: "I didn't know it was on fire!"

3. You know what you call a pig that does karate?
A pork chop

4. You hear what the elephant said to the naked man? He said, "How do you Breathe through something so small?"

5. Why couldn't the leopard play hide and seek?
Because he was always spotted

6. How do you count cows?
With a cowculator

7. Can a kangaroo jump higher than the Empire State Building?
Of course! The Empire State Building cannot jump.

8. What did the duck say when he bought lipstick?
He said, "Put it on my bill."

9. You hear the frog's car broke down?
Yeah, it had to be toad away.

10. You know what is smarter than a talking bird?
A spelling bee

11. Girl: "Dad, why is a swordfish's nose 11 inches long?"
Dad: "Cause if it were 12 inches long, it would be a foot!"

12. What do you call a rabbit that has fleas?
Bugs bunny

13. Did you see they made round bales of hay illegal in Wisconsin?
It's because the cows were not getting a square meal.

14. Why did the crab never share?
Because he is shellfish

15. What did the buffalo say to his son when he dropped him off at school? "Bison."

16. What do you call a deer with no eyes?
No idea

17. You know what the loudest pet you can get is?
A trumpet

18. What do you call a fish with two knees?
A "two-knee" fish

19. What do you call a dog that can do magic?
A Labracadabrador

20. How many tickles does it take to make an octopus laugh?
Ten-tickles

21. What do you get when you cross an elephant with a rhino?
Elephino.

22. When another fish tries to make you think you are cray-zy, tell them to stop Bass-lighting.

23. A three-legged dog walks into a bar and says to the bartender, "I am looking for the man who shot my paw."

24. Why do chicken coops only have two doors?
If they had four, they would be chicken sedans!

25. What did the horse say after it tripped?
"Help! I have fallen, and I can't giddyup!"

26. What do you call a sleeping bull?
A bulldozer

27. Surfing the net is great, unless, of course, you are a fish.

28. Why did the chicken cross the playground?
To get to the other slide

29. What do you get when you cross a fish and an elephant?
Swimming trunks

30. What is the difference between a guitar and a fish?
You can tune a guitar, but you can't tuna fish.

31. What type of sandals do frogs wear?
Open-toad

32. Why couldn't the leopard play hide and seek?
Because he was always spotted

33. Never fall in love with a blowfish.
You will always get re-puffed.

34. When your fish boss is watching, you'd better look e-fish-ent.

35. The thing about calamari is you can never tell when it's just squidding.

36. When jellyfish act catty, it's only because they are jelly.

37. Why are tigers terrible storytellers?
Because they only have one tail

38. What kind of snake would you find on a car?
A windshield viper

39. What kind of bird works at a construction site?
A crane

40. What is orange and sounds like a parrot?
A carrot

41. Why did the cow cross the road?
Because it wanted to go to the mooooovies

42. What do you call a bear with no socks on?
Bare foot

43. Knock knock
Who's there?
Kitten
Kitten who?
You gotta be kitten me!

44. What do you call an older bear who lost his dentures?
A gummy bear

45. What's the ducks favorite meal?
Cheese and quackers

46. What do you call a rabbit that gets stung by a bee?
A honey bunny

47. Why did the cow start becoming mean to the other cows?
Because he was in a baaaad moooood

48. Why do you never see elephants hiding in trees?
Because they are so good at it

49. What do you call a duck who is addicted to drugs?
A quackhead

50. Why did the pigs tail like waking up at 6 AM?
Because it's twirly (too early)

One of my all-time favorite animal dad jokes is:

What are goose bumps for?

To slow the geese down.

A colleague at work shared this joke over lunch one day, and I was in fits. My colleague and I were laughing when another colleague walked in and looked at us funny. I am sure he must be wondering what we thought was so funny on a Monday. Since then, I have repeated this joke countless times, and it never fails to get the intended reaction I want—laughter and sometimes eye rolls (mostly from the younger generation).

Now that you have an entire bag full of animal jokes, enough to entertain an entire zoo, go on and entertain!

In the next chapter, I will share jokes on the family.

4

MAKING FUN OF THE FAMILY

While our family is sacred and we love and respect them, they are also fun to joke around with. They are a great audience, and you can crack a joke with them on any occasion. Whether it's Thanksgiving, Christmas, or Easter, jokes make the mood more festive and lighter. Sometimes the recipients of your jokes will be your uncle, aunt, cousins, siblings, nephews, nieces, and so on. We never know who the lucky winner of our dad jokes will be.

Who do you love cracking jokes with in your family besides your children? Apart from dad jokes, we also have "Yo mama" jokes, which can be used at family occasions, assuming they are not offensive. According to Urban Dictionary these jokes contain a "yo mama" phrase which typically entails a "description of your mother being so 'something' that 'something' occurred as a result" (*Urban Dictionary*, n.d.).

Did you know that "Yo mama" jokes date back before the 21st century? Yes, this might come as a bit of shocker. They were first discovered 3,500 years ago! Yes, I know that is a very long time ago. I am surprised to know people were cracking jokes back then, but good for them! Humor has evolved for the better since the Babylonian times. Thankfully, we don't just include our sweet mother as the butt of the jokes but all our family members, including the dad himself; after all, we don't want anyone to feel left out do we?

The top 50 family dad jokes are:

1. My wife said I should do lunges to stay in shape.
This is a big step forward.

2. What did the baby corn say to the mom corn?
Where's the popcorn?

3. Why do dads feel the need to tell such bad jokes?
They just want to help you become a groan-up.

4. Dad, can you put my shoes on?
No, I don't think they will fit me.

5. When does a joke become a dad joke?
When it becomes apparent.

6. I asked my mom what I could get her for Mother's Day.
She said she'd really like a doctor for a son-in-law.

7. Hell hath no fury like a mother who just caught her kid setting the dinner table with the good dishes.

8. Mom: (Noun) Person who does the work of twenty—for free.

9. To Mom: "I don't feel good" "Where is my sock?" "Will you make me a sandwich?" To Dad: "Where is Mom?"

10. Why is a computer so smart?
It listens to its motherboard.

11. A kid asks his dad, "What is a man?"
The dad says, "A man is someone who is responsible and cares for their family."
The kid replies, "I hope one day I can be a man just like mom!"

12. Sweater: Something you wear when your mom gets cold.

13. Sunday school teacher: "Tell me. Do you say prayers before eating?"
Kid: "No, ma'am, I don't have to. My mom is a good cook."

14. I saw Mommy asking Santa why he didn't put his dishes in the dishwasher.

15. It's not easy being a mom. If it were, dads would do it.

16. Mom logic: If you fall out of that tree and break your legs, don't come running to me!

17. What three words can solve all of Dad's problems?
"Ask your mother."

18. Daughter: "Mom, what is it like to have the greatest daughter in the world?"
Mom: "I don't know. You will have to ask grandma."

19. Wife: "In my dream, I saw you in a jewelry store, and you bought me a diamond ring."
Husband: "I had the same dream, and I saw your dad paying the bill."

20. Why did the can crusher quit his job?
Because it was soda pressing

21. Can February march?
No, but April may

22. How do you make a tissue dance?
Put a little boogie in it.

23. If your uncle has 13 apples in one hand and 10 oranges in the other, what does he have?
Big hands

24. Mother: "Are you talking back to me?!"
Son: "Well yeah, that is kind of how communication works."

25. What is the color of the wind?
Blew

26. Wow! Cory, you sure got tall. I hope you don't grow another foot."
"Why not, Granddad?"
"Because if you do, Mommy will need to buy you a third sneaker."

27. "Granddad, you look pretty sharp with this new haircut. Where did you get your haircut?"
"On my head."

28. You have a hole in your sock, Aunt."
"No, I don't."
"Sure you do. That is how you got your foot in it."

29. Who is a penguin's favorite aunt?
Aunt Arctica

30. Why was the baby ant confused?
Because all his uncles were ants

31. What did auntie Jemima say when she ran out of pancakes?
"How waffle!"

32. My girlfriend is a sniper, but I know she loves me. You know how?
She said she missed me.

33. What did 50 cent say to his grandma after she gifted him a sweater?
G—U Knit?

34. Once my mother advised me on sewing, "As you sew, so shall you rip."

35. My husband was on pins and needles when I reached the final round in a sewing competition.

36. My mother was sewing a quilt for me and asked how it was, but I refused to make a blanket statement.

37. When I was ill, my mother woke up in the middle of the night and cleaned me up. She is a real night towel.

38. My room had no heater, so my mother told me to keep plenty of blankets.
I told her that I had it all covered already.

39. Why did Grandpa's origami business go out?
Because it folded

40. Why did Dad put wheels on Grandpa's rocking chair?
Because grandpa wanted to Rock-n-Roll

41. What is the best thing about being 100 years old according to Grandma? Grandma said, "one gets to live without peer pressure."

42. Why are grandparents and grandchildren always close to each other?
They both have a common enemy at the home front who makes a fuss about eating sweets.

43. Why did grandpa like an "all-you-can-eat" restaurant more than grandma's cooking?
Because he could decide when he was full at the restaurant

44. Why did Grandpa love Grandma so much that he called her love, honey, and darling even after 60 years of marriage?
Because grandpa had forgotten grandma's name

45. Why did the grandchild call his grandpa a hipster?
His grandma told him, hipsters buy clothes from thrift shops, wear glasses that are thick, and look different.

46. Why was Grandma arrested for taking a picture?
She was framed.

47. Why did Grandma stay up all night?
She wanted to see where the sun went. The next day, it dawned on her.

48. Why did the grandma ask her grandson not to work at the candle factory?
He would have to work even on wick-ends.

49. What did the grandma reply when her confused grandson asked her about cloning?
She replied, "I don't know dear, and that will make two of us."

50. What did the grandmother say when her granddaughter asked her about her cat's condition?

Grandma replied, "The cat is f-el-ine now."

I am going to throw in some "Yo mama" jokes for some humor as well!

1. Yo mama's so old, I told her to act her age, and she died.
2. Yo mama's so old, she was Eve.
3. Yo mama's so old, she remembers Fifty Cent when he was a penny.
4. Yo mama's so fat, she jumped in the pool, and they found water on Mars.
5. Yo mama's so poor, ducks throw bread at her.
6. Yo mama's so depressing, blues singers come to visit her when they have writer's block.
7. Yo mama's teeth are so yellow, I can't believe it's not butter.
8. Yo mama's so lazy, she stuck her nose out the window and let the wind blow it.
9. Yo mama's so scary, the government moved Halloween to her birthday.
10. Yo mama's so old, she walked out of a museum, and the alarm went off.

Read the room before cracking "Yo mama" jokes. Sometimes they don't land well with people, for obvious reasons. Do test the waters before jumping into this category of jokes; you don't want to end up in a scuffle over this. I mean, we are looking for laughs, not fights.

One day while I was telling Ava a dad joke, she stopped me midway and said, "Dad I have a joke for you." This made me extremely happy, and I realized my talent had seeped into my daughters, and the generational humor would carry on. She looked at me innocently—mind you, she was 8 years old—and said, "Why do dads feel the need to tell such bad jokes? They just want to help you become a groan-up." I laughed out loud; it was such an adorable moment! Hence, this is one of my favorite family jokes.

At any family occasion, each person should have a huge bag of dad jokes that can fill awkward silences, dissipate a heated discussion, put a smile on everyone's face, and make everyone laugh. Life is too short to be taken so seriously all the time. What's your favorite family and "Yo mama" joke? Leave your favorite joke in the review section.

In the next chapter, I will share jokes on something everyone loves and enjoys—food.

5

FOOD FOR THOUGHT

I love food! Let's be honest, who doesn't? You know that saying, "Live to eat or eat to live?" Well, I live to eat. I also live to joke, and joking about food is fun! Two of my favorite things, apart from my daughters.

From fruit and vegetables to meat and sauces, mealtimes will fall within this funny food chapter. Within this category are some popular dad jokes that have been overused and should be avoided, such as, "I'm on a seafood diet. I see food, I eat food." Maybe it's time to have a look at some new food jokes. What do you think?

It's easy to tell a great dad joke at mealtimes, more so if it's relevant to the food you are eating. These are the times you will often get a greater laugh…or sigh! You may even be met with dead silence. That doesn't stop us from going on. I just want to put it out there once and for all, jokers and comedians need to have patience and perseverance. Even when you are met with awkward silence, don't give up, my friend!

Meal times are when everyone is gathered around the table, there is a sense of togetherness, conversation usually flows, and adding in a joke or two to the mix makes it fun. Moreover, if the mealtime is awkward, or stressful in case of a conflict (especially those annual family Christmas and Thanksgiving dinners where you meet the most distant relatives after months), then you can make the mood lighter or break the ice by cracking a joke. Plus, everyone loves food, so who wouldn't appreciate a good food joke?

The top 50 food themed dad jokes are:

1. A balanced diet is a taco in both hands.

2. A friend got some vinegar in his ear, and now he has pickled hearing.

3. A hangover is the wrath of grapes.

4. A man walked into a bar and ordered a stiff drink. I gave him a glass of ice.

5. A strawberry-growing friend's fruit and vegetable business has gone into liquidation. They make smoothies.

6. Becoming a vegetarian is a huge, missed steak.

7. Candy is nature's way of making up for Mondays.

8. Don't eat someone else's cheesy chips. They are nachos.

9. Don't tell me to stop eating so many tacos. I don't need that kind of negativity in my life.

10. Don't use "beef stew" as a computer password.
It's not stroganoff.

11. Every girl is just like a pineapple: They both have many pointy defenses, but they are still sweet and adorable.

12. Every time I take a drink from a bottle, it keeps pouring back.
It must be spring water.

13. Farmers are real experts; they are often outstanding in their fields.

14. I'm going to a recycling party this weekend. The invite said to bring a bottle.

15. Grain farmers have a tough life.
They barley survive from wheat to wheat.

16. Had too much wine last night.
I have no idea how I got home from the sofa.

17. He said his non-alcoholic wine was delicious. I told him he had zero proof.

18. I accidentally dropped a full two-liter bottle of ginger ale onto my bare foot. Fortunately, it was a soft drink.

19. I almost secretly married a watermelon, but I cantaloupe.

20. I always take life with a grain of salt, plus a slice of lemon, and a shot of tequila.

21. I eat cake every day because it's someone's birthday somewhere out there, and I like celebrating it.

22. I got hit in the head with a can of soda yesterday.
Luckily for me, it was a soft drink.

23. I had Mediterranean food for breakfast, now I falafel.

24. I have always admired fishermen.
They are reel men.

25. I have the best pancake mix!
No, mine is batter!

26. I just stepped on a cornflake.
Now, I am officially a cereal killer.

27. I know it's early, but I am already thinking about tacos.

28. I like to keep my Thanksgiving dinner simple: turkey, stuffing, mashed potatoes, and veggies.
Everything else is just gravy!

29. I love being a butcher.
It makes it easy to meat people.

30. I tried experimenting with spices the other day.
It turned out to be a waste of thyme.

31. What do you call a cow with no legs?
Ground beef

32. What did Bacon say to Tomato?
Lettuce get together.

33. Why did the students eat their homework?
The teacher said that it was a piece of cake.

34. Why did the tomato turn red?
It saw the salad dressing.

35. What did the burger name her daughter?
Patty

36. What do you give to a sick lemon?
Lemon aid

37. What cheese is made backwards?
Edam

38. Why was the mushroom invited to the party?
Because he is a fun-guy

39. How do you make a gold soup?
You put 24 carrots in it.

40. What did the baby corn say to the mama corn?
Where is pop?

41. What is a computer's favorite food?
Micro-chips

42. What kind of sandwich stinks?
A peanut butter and smelly

43. Why did the banana take some medicine?
Because he was not peeling well

44. What is the best food to eat at the post office?
A water mail-in

45. What kind of food do kids eat when they want to celebrate?
Confetti and meatballs

46. What do you call a strawberry that likes to spin?
A berry go round

47. What is the funniest candy bar?
Snickers

48. I would do a steak joke, but they are never well done.

49. What do you call it when two chips fall in love?
A relation-dip

50. Who is the best kung-fu vegetable?
Brocc Lee

My angels and I were having dinner one night. We had ordered in pizza and ice-cream (it was a treat day). Everyone was hungrily gobbling on their cheese pizza, and we aren't allowed to talk while chewing. I decided to crack a joke, because why not? I asked them, "If a turkey runs away, does that make it a chicken?" At first they were confused, but then they started giggling. Though Mia did require some explaining, which Mercy did on my behalf. The lesson I learned from this was that you should know your audience's age and comprehension abilities before picking a joke. My prime audience is my daughters, so I have a lot of children friendly and easy to understand jokes up my sleeve.

Food jokes don't necessarily have to be cracked at the dinner table, you can tell them anywhere! I believe in not limiting food jokes to over dinner or career jokes to the office—variety is the spice of life.

In the next chapter, I will share jokes on the body, but don't worry. They are not mean and rude ones. They are easy going and lame ones.

6

WHOLE BODY GIGGLES

Nobody is perfect, and we all have flaws. A lot of jokes are centered on these flaws, which can be insensitive! Even though these are light-hearted jokes, always check your audience, especially if your kids are sensitive about a physical aspect. Dad jokes can go horribly wrong when you mention a 12-inch long nose to someone paranoid about their nose! So, while we love being funny, poking fun at each other, and making the moment lighthearted, it's also important to be mindful and sensitive. It's the 21st century, and we have become aware and progressed from racist, fat-shaming, and mean jokes. This is just a small reminder to be a mindful comedian!

The top 50 body dad jokes are:

1. What do you call a tower made of body parts?
Body building

2. Why does the nose like to be in the middle of the face?
It likes to be the center of attention.

3. Why are the eyes considered to be the last organ to die?
Because pupils die-late

4. What did an eye say to the other eye?
You know, there is something between the both of us that smells.

5. What is the fastest thing on your face?
Your nose (It's always running.)

6. What did the skeleton order for dinner?
Spareribs

7. What did the left hand ask the right hand?
How can you always be right?

8. Why does the heart listen to a lot of dance music?
Because it loves feeling the beat

9. What happens to a bear with a bad heart?
It goes into Kodiak arrest.

10. What is the quickest way to a man's heart?
Through his chest

11. What does a pirate with heart failure need?
He needs anti-arrrrrrrrrrhythmics.

12. What causes black-belt heart attacks?
Karate-d arteries

13. What do you call a dancer from Ireland having a heart attack?
Michael Flatline

14. What did the skeleton say to his girlfriend?
I love every bone in your body!

15. What do you find inside a clean nose?
Fingerprints

16. What has a bottom at the top?
Your legs

17. What nails do carpenters hate hammering?
Fingernails

18. Why did the foot smile?
He was toe happy

19. Why did the skeleton cross the road?
Because it had to go to the Body Shop

20. Why didn't the skeleton dance?
Because he had no body to dance with

21. Why was the nose feeling sad?
It was tired of getting picked on.

22. What makes music on your hair?
A head band

23. What do you call a man without a body and a nose?
Nobody nose

24. My 9-year-old son has started asking awkward questions about the human body...
I suppose the freezer was not the best place to hide it.

25. It's true. A lot of people are only after me for my body.
Kidneys, liver, heart, and lungs

26. Which body part is the most reliable?
Fingers because you can always count on them

27. Which is the most desired summer body this year?
The antibody

28. My wife just recently completed a 40-week body building course.
It's a baby boy, and he weighs 11lbs 4oz.

29. What smells the best at dinner?
Your nose

30. Did you pick your nose?
No, I was born with it!

31. I love my legs because they always stand up for me.

32. Breaking a leg while auditioning will ensure that you make it in the cast.

33. What did the left hand ask the right hand? How can you always be right?

34. What did the lips say to the facial muscle? You always make me smile.

35. What is the quickest way to a man's heart? Through his chest

36. What did the barber say when he shaved someone's thick hair?
He said, "Hair comes trouble!"

37. Why did my young daughter put a bun on her hair?
Because her mother had told her to tie a bun

38. One arm told another arm a joke.
The other arm found the joke very humerus.

39. What do arms do when you get sad?
They give you a shoulder to cry on.

40. Why should you always thank your arms?
For always being by your side

41. What button is impossible to button?
The belly button

42. What did the skeleton get from his office after doing all the good works?
A bone-us

43. I got my arm transplant done at a great money price yesterday.
It sure was discounted at the second-hand store.

44. I wanted to look cool at my friend's dance class, so I said anyone can do a handstand.
When the teacher asked me to do it, I asked my friend to place his hand on the floor and I merely stood on it.

45. My sister broke her fingers after an accident. When the doctor came in and asked her a question about how she was feeling now, she said, "With my elbows mostly."

46. Everyone is always telling me to follow my heart, but I am not sure what "boomboom, boomboom" means.

47. I saw a skeleton playing football, but he couldn't score any goals: his heart just was not in it.

48. Skeletons are known to be extremely lonely in general because they have no body!

49. My sister fractured two fingers on her left-hand today.
On the other hand, everything is fine.

50. There was a skeleton who was a botanist.
His favorite kind of tree was a bone-zai tree.

Jokes about one's appearance and body don't have to necessarily be mean and rude. They can also be lame, friendly, and sensitive! I have provided you with a list of them, so you can get started.

One day, I pretended to pick my nose (on purpose, so don't judge me) in front of my daughters, and the obvious reaction I received was, "Eww daddy, did you just pick your nose?"

To which I responded, "No honey, I was born with it."

Do you see what I did there? I set them up to crack my joke rather than asking them straight forward. Most times, you can be inventive in relating the joke. Don't be afraid to be creative. Safety and reservations don't work too well with humor. Tell me which comedian you have come across who has not offended at least one person or not been creative?

There are numerous body jokes which can be used to ease a tense situation like waiting for a doctor, dentist, or hospital appointment. Use a kid's dad joke to explain how you helped your child relax in the waiting room. I have tried this with my daughters when they had to go for their vaccinations. All children and so many adults are scared of injections, so it helps ease the anxiety if you crack a joke here and there. Here is one you can tell your children, "What did the vampire doctor shout out in his waiting room? Necks, please!"

In the next chapter, I will share jokes on pop culture for every age bracket.

7

CRACKS ABOUT POP CULTURE

Pop culture includes all jokes relating to music, TV, fashion, dance, art, literature, film, and even cyber culture. Though the pop is short for popular, don't forget pop culture for the different generations. Your audience is diverse.

Politicians are the punch line to many jokes, but we will leave those to social media. From Harry Potter to Lady Gaga, dads will get a laughing reaction with the following jokes. There also some jokes that are not child appropriate in the following list, so be careful when you are relating to these children, we are keeping it R-rated here!

The top 50 pop culture dad jokes are:

1. Women call me ugly occasionally, but that is only until they hear how much money I make. Then, they say I am poor and ugly.

2. Why did Adele cross the road?
To sing, "Hello from the other side!"

3. What computer sings the best?
A Dell

4. If you want a list of Chuck Norris' enemies, just check the extinct species list.

5. Why do blonde girls walk in groups of odd numbers?
Because they can't even

6. What is the Mexican version of One Direction?
Juan Direction

7. What do you call an ocean voyage where everyone stays in the closet?
A Tom Cruise

8. What did Obi-Wan say to Luke at the breakfast table?
"Use the fork, Luke."

9. Why does Helen Keller have holes in her face?
She tried eating with a fork.

10. Evolution is a list of things Chuck Norris let live.

11. I left my Adderall in my Ford Fiesta, now it's a Ford Focus.

12. Why did the zombie want to eat Meghan Trainor?
Every inch of her was perfect from the bottom to the top.

13. What college does Kim Kardashian's daughter want to attend when she grows up?
Northwestern

14. Why did the shark cross the road?
To get to the other tide

15. Chuck Norris doesn't sleep, he waits.

16. What is the difference between Tiger Woods and Santa Claus?
Santa stops after three ho's.

17. Kids wear Superman pajamas; Superman wears Chuck Norris pajamas.

18. How do you find Will Smith in a snow storm?
You follow the fresh prints.

19. What do you call Cardi B on a treadmill?
Cardi O

20. Why did Blake Shelton break up with Miranda Lambert?
Her lips didn't taste like sangria!

21. Did anyone hear about George Clooney's new genealogical website?
It's called, "Oh, Brother Where Art Thou."

22. Why does the NSA hate blizzards?
Because they get Snowden

23. Where do the Burger King and Dairy Queen live?
At the White Castle

24. How much coke has Charlie Sheen snorted?
Enough to kill two and a half men

25. Is it safe to swim in the ocean this week?
Sure, the sharks are all busy filming with Discovery.

26. What kind of name would Miley Cyrus and Terminator gave to their first baby?
The Twerkinator

27. Why did Captain Kirk go in to the ladies room?
He wanted to go where no man had gone before.

28. What did Elvis say after he was bitten by a vampire?
Fang you, Fang you very much!

29. What do you call 5 gay guys walking straight?
One Direction

30. Why is Peter Pan always flying?
Because he neverlands

31. What did Jay-Z call his girlfriend before getting married?
Feyoncè

32. What show do cows love to watch while they are eating?
Graze Anatomy

33. Why did Papa Smurf send Smurfette to see a doctor?
She was always feeling blue.

34. A politician will find an excuse to get out of anything except office.

35. Which singer is the best at fixing things?
Shawn Mendes

36. Which actress never uses cutlery?
Reese Without-a-spoon

37. Which coffee is the most famous?
Ariana Grande

38. Which singer is good with hairstyles?
Harry Styles

39. Which rapper takes the most naps?
Jay Zzzzzzz

40. How did Barack Obama propose to Michelle Obama?
He got down on one knee, pulled out a ring, and said "I don't wanna be Obamaself."

41. How do you cure hunger in Minecraft?
Three square meals

42. What do you call a Minecraft celebration?
A block party

43. What did the jam say to Beyonce?
I don't think you're ready for this jelly.

44. What do you call it when Erykah Badu falls down the stairs?
Erykah Badu, Badu, Badu

45. What had luxurious alpaca fur and drops classic albums?
Kendrick Llama

46. What soulful singer helped my cut my paper in half?
SZA

47. What advice did Biggie Smalls give to the cow?
Moo money, moo problems

48. What is Forrest Gump's Wi Fi password?
1Forest1

49. What did Ja-Rule use to sign the hit man's contract?
Murder ink

50. What kind of horse does Kim Kardashian ride?
Kan-neigh

Because I am such a joker myself, my daughters have picked up the same trait from me. Hence, I am not the only one cracking jokes in the house. Mercy, who is 10 years old, is the most equipped with jokes since she is the oldest. She cracks pop culture jokes from time to time, and sometimes they go right over my head because I have no clue what she is referring to, and the humor is lost. I then ask her to explain it to me, and she just rolls her eyes and says, "dad you will not understand, you are old." I can't argue with that.

For instance, she asked me, "How do you respect BTS?" The answer was "You bow wow wow." I knew who this was referring to because Mercy listens to their songs. They are a South Korean boy band. I definitely will not be cracking BTS jokes with my friends. She overheard this one at school, not through me!

Pop culture is generally only funny when the listener knows the subject, so choose your audience wisely. I will not be cracking Chuck Norris jokes with my daughters. I am sure they will look at me funny and say, "Who?"

In the next chapter I will share jokes on jobs and careers.

8

JESTING ABOUT JOBS

Some of the funnier classics are jokes about the doctor. However, there are a good number of gardener, financial, psychologist, and athlete jokes as well. Life doesn't end with doctor jokes; I just want to put it out there. Let us learn to laugh about other careers as well.

These dad jokes I will share with you are perfect for a few groans and giggles in the office. There is nothing wrong with being the funny guy or gal in the workplace. Plus, for those with adult children, a work joke from dad can ease the day's tension.

The top 50 career dad jokes are:

1. I just lost my job as a psychic.
I did not see that coming.

2. Hard work pays off in the future, laziness pays off now.

3. I am looking for a job where I am politely ignored and left to my own devices. With unlimited Internet access, doughnuts, and coffee.

4. Now I have gotten into astronomy, and my whole career is looking up.

5. I quit my job working for Nike.
I just couldn't do it anymore.

6. I quit my job at the helium factory.
I refuse to be spoken to in that tone!

7. I love being a maze designer.
I get completely lost in my work.

8. I wanted to be a computer programmer, but I couldn't hack it.

9. I wanted to be a pet groomer, but I couldn't make heads or tails of it.

10. I got a job as a human cannonball.
It was a high-caliber position, but I had a short fuse and got fired!

11. Inspecting mirrors is a job I could really see myself doing.

12. Sure, I am willing to work longer hours at work.
as long as they are lunch hours

13. I think my job interview to be a bug sorter went well.
I boxed all the right ticks.

14. Interviewer: "What is your biggest weakness?"
Me: "I don't know when to quit."
Interviewer: "You are hired."
Me: "I quit."

15. My best job was being a musician, but eventually, I found I wasn't noteworthy.

16. I studied a long time to become a doctor, but I did not have any patients.

17. I became a professional fisherman but discovered that I couldn't live on my net income.

18. I thought about becoming a witch, so I tried that for a spell.

19. I am aspirin' to be a chemist.

20. I wanted to be a tree doctor, but I faint at the sight of sap.

21. I managed to get a good job working for a pool maintenance company, but the work was just too draining.

22. I wanted to get into the engineering field, but I burned too many bridges.

23. I got a job at a zoo feeding giraffes, but I was fired because I was not up to it.

24. I got fired as a yoga instructor, and I bent over backwards for those people!

25. I thought about being a knife-maker.
I made great blades, but I just couldn't handle it.

26. I found being an electrician interesting, but the work was shocking.

27. I got fired from the unemployment office and still had to show up the next day.

28. After many years of trying to find steady work, I finally got a job as a historian, until I realized there was no future in it.

29. I applied for a job in Australia, but it seems I don't have the right koalifications.

30. I worked at Krispy Kreme, but I quickly got fed up with the hole business.

31. Rumors are that the software developer went bankrupt.
It may be because he used up all his cache.

32. The owner of the pest control agency is very religious.
He likes to motivate his employees by s-praying.

33. I asked the train engineer why he got fired. "Management says I have a one track mind," was his reply.

34. It's funny that even the headhunter couldn't find a job for my musician friend. Maybe it's because he is not note-worthy.

35. My wife is a skilled X-ray technician.
It's funny how she always sees right through my lies.

36. Why should you never steal a photographer's lens?
He will remember you because he has a photographic memory.

37. Why did the camera stop dreaming about a career in photography?
He couldn't remain focused.

38. Why do firefighters like the summer?
They are used to the heat!

39. What happened to the firefighter who was not doing well in his job?
He got fired!

40. Doctor, doctor! I get heartburn whenever I eat birthday cake.
Next time, take the candles off!

41. What do you call a female magician in the desert?
A sand-witch

42. Why did the doctor become angry?
He ran out of patience.

43. What candy made the astronaut sad?
Starburst

44. What did DJ Allergies say to the nose?
Why don't you drop it like its snot?

45. What did the janitor say when he jumped out of the closet?
Supplies!

46. Did you hear about the lumberjack who got fired for cutting down too many trees?
He saw too much.

47. What do you call a marathon for pastors?
A rev-run

48. My friend recently got her real estate license. Now she's my home girl.

49. Why did the gangster have to keep seeing the eye doctor?
He had Glock-oma.

50. My dentist is a mean guy!
He always hurts my fillings.

Here is one for all the authors and writers out there. "If Moses were alive today, he would come down from the mountain with the Ten Commandments and spend the next five years trying to get them published." I feel that, since I am a writer as well. Pulling each other's legs about what we do is always fun. Since jobs can get monotonous, we might as well have a good laugh about the monotony.

If you haven't guessed by now, I am the office comedian, and I keep the office staff laughing from time to time.

In the next chapter, I will share everything hobby related.

9

HORSING AROUND WITH HOBBIES

This chapter will include all sorts of jokes about the hobbies that we take up. Of all the possible hobbies, my favorites are playing with my daughters, cooking their dinner, watching them play sports, reading them a bedtime story, and of course, making them laugh. Go ahead and choose any joke to crack with your loved ones about their favorite hobbies.

The top 50 hobby-related dad jokes are:

1. I used to like origami, but I gave up as there was too much paperwork.

2. My hobbies are knitting and swimming, but the wool gets soggy.

3. I needed a hobby, so I decided to take up fencing.
My neighbors were furious.

4. What time do tennis players go to bed?
Tennish

5. What lights up a football pitch at night?
A football match

6. Why didn't the dog play football?
It was a boxer.

7. I just started baking lessons.
Up till now, it's a piece of cake.

8. My exercising equipment has a hobby.
It collects dust.

9. My Dad grows herbs as a hobby.
He has too much Thyme on his hands.

10. I took up picking locks as a hobby.
It has opened a lot of doors for me.

11. Every day, I spend a few hours on a running machine.
Next week, I might even turn it on.

12. My hobby was skiing, but it went downhill fast.

13. Did you hear about the skydiving club that closed?
The members kept falling out.

14. I was thinking of doing yoga, so I called the leisure center. They asked me if I was flexible.
I said, "Yes, I can do anytime except for Tuesday's."

15. We moved our treadmill outside, so I can smoke.

16. I used to work for an origami company until it folded.

17. I took up snail racing as a hobby.
I thought removing their shells would make them go faster, but it just made them sluggish.

18. As a hobby, I started taking walks around the old clock tower.
It's a great way to pass the time.

19. You need to be so careful when you are hot air ballooning.
It's easy to get carried away.

20. My hobby used to be whale watching.
I gave it up because I just couldn't see the porpoise.

21. What is a spider's favorite hobby?
Surfing the web

22. Did you hear about the overweight man who spent his spare time in a casino?
He heard it was the quickest way to lose pounds.

23. I tried water polo, but my horse drowned.

24. I recently took up blindfold archery.
I didn't know what I was missing.

25. Today, a man knocked on my door and asked for a small donation towards the local swimming pool.
I gave him a glass of water.

26. Doing yoga got me out of the habit of biting my fingernails.
Now I bite my toenails.

27. If you win three games of Twister in a row, you are automatically a yoga instructor.

28. What does Iron Man do in his spare time?
He irons clothes.

29. What android team won the Olympic water sports?
The rowbots!

30. I went to a climbing club the other day, but someone had stolen all the grips from the wall.
You couldn't make it up.

31. I had an art contest with my friend.
It ended in a draw.

32. I missed a couple of my cooking classes.
Now, I have some ketchup to do.

33. Why do we paint Easter eggs?
It's easier than trying to wallpaper them.

34. Why did the ants dance on jam jars?
The label said, "twist to open."

35. I used to make furniture out of plants.
It was no bed of roses.

36. How many line dance instructors does it take to change a light bulb?
Five!…Six!…Seven!…Eight!

37. I named my dog Miles, so I can tell people that I walk Miles every single day.

38. A friend of mine collects blunt pencils.
I find that a bit pointless.

39. What is the hardest thing about learning to ride a bike?
The ground

40. I am great at identifying birds.
Okay, what are those in that tee?
Yes, they are definitely all birds.

41. I was addicted to the hokey pokey, but luckily, I turned myself around.

42. My dad has this weird hobby where he collects modern bottles.
That sounds way better than alcoholic.

43. Sharing these swimming puns at a summer pool party is the perfect way to have pun in the sun.

44. I thought of learning sewing, but I did not have all the equipment.
Needle-ss to say, I did not reach any further.

45. What does the gardener do when spring arrives?
They wet their plants.

46. Sometimes swimming is hard work, and sometimes it's easy.
It deep-ends.

47. If Shakespeare writes a play on sewing, he would name it: *To Sew Or Not To Sew.*

48. What are the kinds of socks a gardener wears?
Garden hose

49. Swimmers try to stay away from dark chocolate because, according to studies, it lowers the chances of a stroke.

50. People who sew are lucky; they have a Singer in the house.

I really enjoy gardening, it soothes my mind, makes me feel at peace, and I have a green thumb. I even grow my own vegetables in a small vegetable patch. I make sure to get my daughters involved whenever I am planting a new seed, so they can also see how fun and satisfactory it is to see a seed turn into a plant and the journey of blooming.

One day, while my daughters and I were planting flower seeds, they spotted a honeybee and began screaming in fear. I shooed it away, but to turn the moment lighter and dissipate their fear, I told the following joke:

"What would a bee say to the flower? Hello honey."

They laughed, nervously. Because I sensed that the joke worked, I told them another one:

"What kind of flowers grow in outer space? Sunflowers."

The second joke eased them further, and we got back to our initial activity of planting flower seeds.

What is your favorite hobby? What are your children's favorite hobbies? You can build jokes around those particular hobbies.

In the next chapter, I will share jokes on everything education and academic related.

10

THE ESCAPADES OF EDUCATION

Did you know, that 15% of our lifetime is spent in school? ("What Percentage of the Average Life of an American Is Spent at School?," 2015). This includes the time from kindergarten to 12th grade. That is a lot of time over an average lifespan. So, when a child feels like their entire day is spent at school, they have a valid reason to feel that way. Moreover, they even have homework, test preparations, and so on. There will be days when your child will not want to go to school, do their homework, or wake up early for school. You might as well use those opportunities to crack some educational jokes and motivate them.

Who knows? Your child may repeat the joke to someone else for motivational reasons! In a way, you end up promoting literacy. There are a range of educational and school jokes for children. I will divide them between children, teens, and teachers as well, because they are an essential part of education!

The top 50 education dad jokes are:

1. Dad: "Can I see your report card, son?"
Son: "I don't have it."
Dad: "Why?"
Son: "I gave it to my friend. He wanted to scare his parents."

2. Teacher: "What is the value of Pi?"
Student: "Depending on what pie, it is usually $12.99."

3. Teacher: "Name a bird with wings but can't fly."
Student: "A dead bird, sir."

4. Teacher: "Jill, where is America on the map?"
Jill: "right there"
Teacher: "Correct. Now, Jack, tell me who found America."
Jack: "Jill did."

5. It was the first day of school. Harry's mother went into his bedroom and said, "Come on Harry, get up now. You have to go to school today."
"But I don't want to go to school," replied Harry, "I want to stay in bed. Why do I have to go to school?"
"Because," answered his mother, "you are a teacher!"

6. Why did the girl wear glasses in math class?
It improves di-vision.

7. Friend 1: "You never study, so how come you don't fail your math tests?"
Friend 2: "Because whenever there is a math test, I don't go to school!"

8. What type of exam does the vampire teacher give his students?
A blood test

9. Teacher: "John, why are you doing your math multiplication on the floor?"
John: "You told me to do it without using tables."

10. Chad: "Why do magicians do so well in school?"
Josh: "I don't know. Why?"
Chad: "They are good at trick questions."

11. Jacob: "Why was the teacher wearing sunglasses to school?"
Leonard: "Why?"
Jacob: "She had bright students!"

12. Teacher: "Class, we will have only half a day of school this morning."
Class: "Hooray!"
Teacher: "We will have the other half this afternoon."

13. Teacher: "Donald, what is the chemical formula for water?"
Donald: "H-I-J-K-L-M-N-O"
Teacher: "What are you talking about?"
Donald: "Yesterday you said it was H to O."

14. Teacher: "Daniel, I have had to send you to the principal every day this week. What do you have to say for yourself?"
Daniel: "I'm glad it's Friday!"

15. Phil: "What makes a Cyclops such an effective teacher?"
Cheryl: "I don't know."
Phil: "He has only one pupil."

16. How do you know that you have been in college too long?
Your parents are running out of money!

17. College student: "Hey, Dad—I have some great news for you!"
Father: "What, son?"
College student: "Remember that $500 you promised me if I made the Dean's list?"
Father: "I certainly do."
College student: "Well, you get to keep it!"

18. You can't see a thing when it's foggy in Los Angeles, but once the fog clears U.C L.A.

19. I am a chemistry student, but I am thinking of becoming a comedian because I am so-dium funny.

20. On graduation day, the tallest boy in our class said, "I have graduated at the top of the class."

21. Do you know why people laughed at a grad student when he told everyone about his graduation?
He was graduating from a clown college.

22. The geometry teacher did not come to school today.
I heard she sprained her angle.

23. The math class went on way too long because the teacher kept going off on a tangent.

24. When the students did not pay attention, the science teacher said, "You need to understand the gravity of this science lesson!"

25. It was wrong to kick me out of school after I got married.
I only wanted my bachelor's degree.

26. The school dance was such a joke.
It had a big punch line.

27. Teacher: "Tommy, can you tell us where the Declaration of Independence was signed?"
Tommy: "Yes, at the bottom."

28. Teacher: "Why did you eat your homework, Joe?"
Joe: "I don't have a dog."

29. Johnny: "Teacher, would you punish me for something I did not do?"
Teacher: "Of course not."
Johnny: "Good, because I did not do my homework."

30. What is the difference between an American student and an English student?
about 3,000 miles

31. A woman called the dean of the college that her freshman son was going to.
"I am worried. I don't know who my son can hang out with. He doesn't have the kind of money all the other students have."
The dean replied, "Well then, he can hang out with the faculty."

32. A Geometry teacher's favorite ride at the amusement park is the rulercoaster.

33. The old mother asked her son, "Which were the darkest days of your life you faced?"
He replied, "The college days—I was so broke that I couldn't pay the electricity bill."

34. Whenever I have graph paper, people think I am plotting something.

35. I decided to surprise my parents by visiting from college unannounced—only to find out they'd taken a vacation and not left the keys behind. Not a problem though, all I have to do is talk to the door lock.

36. They always told me, "communication is the key."
One day a college professor, after getting irritated in his college class, stood up in front of the class and asked if anyone in the class was an idiot and said if there was one, then they should stand up.
After a minute, a young man stood up. The professor then asked that guy if he actually thought he was an idiot.
The boy replied, "No, I just did not want to see you standing there all by yourself."

37. All the fraternity brothers left the house for a long weekend except for Grady, who decided to stay behind and get some studying done. One night, Grady heard a noise under his bed. Fearing it might be a burglar, he leaned over and whispered, "Anybody there?"
"No," said the burglar.
"That is funny," the boy said to himself. "I could have sworn I heard a noise!"

38. Teacher to student: "If I give you 3+3 rabbits, how many do you have?"
Student: "I will have 7 rabbits."
Teacher: "How?"
Student: "I already have 1 rabbit."

39. The earth science teacher was giving a lecture on map reading. After explaining latitude, longitude, degrees, and minutes, the teacher said, "Suppose I asked you to meet me for lunch at 23 degrees, four minutes north latitude and 45 degrees, 15 minutes east longitude where would it be?"
After a confused silence, a voice volunteered, "I guess you will be eating alone."

40. Our English teacher seems to be the most logical person among the faculty.
He always uses his comma-sense in a difficult situation.

41. My mom didn't like my report card. I said, "okay."
She said, "I want more A's."
I said, "Okaaaaay!"

42. One time, I told a chemistry joke, but there was no reaction.

43. Nobody heard of the guy who would get into trouble for making puns in school after he was pun-ished.

44. What kind of school do you go to if you are…
…an ice cream man? sundae school
…a giant? high school
…a surfer? boarding school
…King Arthur? knight school

45. Stevie: "Hey, Mom, I got a hundred in school today!"
Mom: "That is great. Which subject?"
Stevie: "A 40 in reading and a 60 in spelling"

46. Nate: "Why was school easier for cave people?"
Kate: "Why?"
Nate: "Because there was no history to study!"

47. The dean of a college told the auditorium, "The female dormitory will be out-of-bounds for all male students, so too, the male dormitory to female students. Anybody caught breaking this rule will be fined $20 the first time. Anybody caught breaking this rule the second time will be fined $60. Being caught a third time will incur a hefty fine of $180. Are there any questions?"
At this, a student in the crowd raised their hand and asked, "Er… how much for a season pass?"

48. Why did the music note drop out of college?
It couldn't pick a major.

49. You should never gift anything to your history teacher.
He will not like the present.

50. Our computer teacher quit teaching school students because he lost his drive.

Depending on your child's age, you can crack whatever joke you think is appropriate. My daughters definitely will not be laughing at college jokes because it would be beyond them, and college aged children will think school jokes are lame. I have also thrown in teacher jokes, so if you happen to be a teacher, I hope you have a good laugh after reading them.

Sometimes when my daughters have a bad day at school, and I can see they are visibly upset, I crack a joke or two to cheer them up. It works sometimes, and sometimes it doesn't, but it's worth the effort. Honestly, school is tough. This is especially true if your child is transitioning into the middle school age life. I know that Mercy will be going to middle school next year and will meet with her fair share of uncomfortable and upsetting incidents (which all teens go through). However, I am certain that during those days I can be there for her, to make her smile or laugh and help her through these changing times.

In the next chapter, I am going to share jokes on holidays, vacations, and road trips!

11

WISECRACKS FOR THE ROAD

Who doesn't love road trips or holidays via plane, bus, or train? They are fun, long, and sometimes monotonous (depending on where you are headed). They can be filled with laughter, chatter, or family and friends time. I love taking road trips and travelling with my daughters. During their summer break, I rent out an RV, and we go to an unexplored location where all of us share the excitement of seeing a new place together for the first time. Even a short plane ride is enough for me to bring out my jokes and pass the time. It's a win-win situation—holidays and laughter.

In this chapter, I will be sharing a lot of jokes on holidays and modes of transport. Whether you are planning your next vacation, sightseeing, or trying to change the subject from, "Are we nearly there yet?" A dad joke will hit the funny spot. I mean come on, holiday, road trip, or plane ride and jokes—can you think of a better combo? I certainly cannot. Remember, these jokes are not just for family road trips, holidays, and vacations, they are jokes for friends as well.

The top 50 road trip dad jokes are:

1. How can you tell elephants love to travel?
They always pack their own trunk!

2. Where do sharks love to go on their holidays?
Finland

3. How do rabbits like to travel?
By hareplane

4. Why did the witch stay in a hotel?
She heard they had great broom service!

5. Where do hamsters go on their holidays?
To Hamsterdam

6. What do you get when you cross a plane with a magician?
A flying sorcerer

7. What happens when you wear a watch on a plane?
Time flies!

8. How do fleas like to travel?
Itch hiking

9. Why did the librarian get chucked off the plane?
It was overbooked!

10. Why are mountains the funniest place to travel to?
They are hill areas!

11. What do you get when you cross a snake with a plane?
A Boeing constrictor

12. What country has the most germs?
Germany

13. Where is a teacher's favorite holiday destination?
Times Square

14. How can you tell a train just went by?
You can see its tracks!

15. What happened to the man who took the five o'clock train home?
He had to give it back!

16. Why is that train engine humming?
It doesn't know the words!

17. If you are on a road trip and you see a fork in the road, what should you do? Stop for lunch!

18. What did the doctor say to the man who was sick at the airport?
It's a terminal illness!

19. Where do pepperonis go on holiday?
The leaning tower of pizza

20. Where do bees go on their holiday?
Stingapore

21. Why is Peter Pan always flying?
He Neverlands!

22. What is the most popular chocolate sold at airports?
Plane chocolate

23. What did E.T.'s mother say to him when he got home?
Where on earth have you been?!

24. Knock, Knock
Who's there?
Europe
Europe who?
No, you are!

25. Knock, Knock
Who's there?
Cargo
Cargo who?
Car go, "beep, beep."

26. Knock, Knock
Who's there?
Hawaii
Hawaii who?
I'm good, Hawaii you?!

27. I would love to go to Holland one day... wooden shoe?

28. I have always wanted to travel to Finland, but I am afraid I might disappear into FinAir!

29. A time traveler went to a restaurant and had the best meal he had ever had.
He liked it so much he went back four seconds!

30. What travels the world but stays in one corner?
A stamp

31. What goes through towns, up hills, and down hills but never moves?
The road

32. What state in the U.S is round at the ends and hi in the middle?
Ohio

33. What can you find in Jupiter, Mercury, Mars, Earth, but not Neptune or Venus?
The letter "R."

34. A bus driver was heading along a busy road and went the wrong way down a one-way street. He went past three stop signs but did not stop, and he spoke to someone on his mobile phone. However, the bus driver didn't break any laws. How was this possible?
The bus driver was walking, not driving!

35. What is the capital of France?
"F"

36. I cannot believe this is the first year I'm not going to Fiji because of COVID-19.
Normally, I don't go because I am poor.

37. Where do sheep go on vacation?
They go to the baaaaaahaaaaaamas.

38. Traveling on a train for too long:
Conductor on a train: "But sir, you cannot travel with this! This is a child's ticket! You are at least 19 years old!"
Backpacker: "You see how horribly long your delays are? You should be ashamed!"

39. When visiting Pompeii in Italy…
What does one volcano say to the other volcano?
"I lava you!"

40. Knock, Knock!
Who's there?
Buck and Ham
Buck and Ham who?
Buck and Ham palace

41. Knock, Knock!
Who's there?
Oscar
Oscar who?
Oscar if she wants to go on the trip with us!

42. When in France…
I will travel to France. Do you know why?
I have nothing Toulouse.

43. When in Thailand…
You know what, PHUKET…I am leaving!

44. I am not sure where to find snow in America.
Alaska local.

45. My wife told me: "Sex is better on vacation."
That was not a very nice postcard to receive.

46. Where do cows go on vacation?
Moo York

47. Why did no one like the airplane?
It had a bad altitude.

48. Why did Mister Krabs not invite Spongebob on vacation?
He is shellfish.

49. A photon is going through airport security.
The TSA agent asks if it has any luggage.
The photon says, "No, I am traveling light."

50. What did the Japanese receptionist say when I was 2 hours late checking into my hotel?
You really Tokyo time.

During my daughters' summer breaks, we decided to go to Switzerland. I have always wanted to visit because of the Swiss Alps, but my daughters were more interested in the chocolate. It was an amazing vacation. We did a lot of nature related activities and sightseeing. One day, we were eating out at a restaurant known for its cheese fondue, and the waitress came to take our order. We started chatting, and she struck up a conversation with my daughters and asked, "What do you like about Switzerland?" I immediately responded (because I knew this was the perfect opportunity for this joke) and said, "Well, the flag is a big plus." I got a loud and appreciative laugh from the waitress, but my daughters just cringed and sank into their seats. Mercy groaned out loud. Oh well, at least I got to crack this joke in its true homeland!

In the next chapter, I will share jokes on STEM.

12

STEM

What does STEM stand for? This stands for science, technology, engineering, and math. This is a technical field my friends! There will be plenty of wordplays related to new technology, but don't forget some of the classics about what is now considered old technology. For instance, I cannot crack a joke with my daughters about a VCR! Those are now considered antique items I am sure. STEM is an excellent source of humor for anyone who struggles with today's technology but also a chance to explore the wittier puns around town.

When one hears STEM, they assume seriousness and rigidity, but let me challenge that assumption with some good STEM jokes. Since some of them may not make sense to you, I will give a disclaimer at the bottom for the ones that may need further explanation. I know, I know, explaining kills the joke, but would you rather not know the joke and laugh about it, rather than just skimming over it saying "what?" Gear up for some technical explanations. At least you will be more knowledgeable about STEM after finishing this chapter, and you can thank me later for that.

The top 50 STEM dad jokes are:

1. A neutron walks into a bar and asks the barman, "How much is it for a drink?" The barman says, "For you, no charge."
Explainer: Neutrons constitute the middle (nucleus) of atoms and don't have any electric charge. They are different from protons (positively charged) and electrons (negatively charged).

2. Did you hear the rumor about oxygen going on a date with potassium?
Well, it went OK.
Explainer: The chemical symbol for oxygen is O and potassium is K.

3. A scientist and his friend walk into a bar. The bartender asks what they would like to drink. The scientist says. "I will have an H_2O."

The friend says, "I will have an H_2O too." The friend dies after sipping on the drink.
Explainer: H_2O is water and H_2O_2 is hydrogen peroxide.
Hydrogen peroxide causes chemical burns and choking.

4. Schrodinger's cat walks into a bar and doesn't!
Explainer: Schrodinger's Cat is a thought experiment in the field of physics. A cat is kept in a box with a radioactive source and poison. The cat is assumed to be both dead and alive until the box is opened.

5. There are two types of people in this world; those who can extrapolate from incomplete data.
Explainer: Extrapolation is estimating what the result may be beyond what you actually measured. The joke is that some people cannot extrapolate from data, hence they cannot work out the ending of the joke—the other type of person.

6. There are 10 types of people in this world; those who understand binary and those who don't.
Explainer: Binary is a method of using two

different symbols, 0 and 1, to represent any number. It's used to generate code for computers. 10 in binary is the same as writing 2. Hence, there are two types of people, those who understand binary and those who don't.

7. Two atoms were walking along, one of them says, "Oh no, I think I have lost an electron!"
"Are you sure?"
"Yes, I am positive."
Explainer: If an atom loses an electron (a negatively charged particle) it becomes positively charged.

8. A group of protestors are protesting in front of a Physics lab, "What do we want?"
"Time travel"
"When do we want it?"
"Irrelevant"
Explainer: If time travel was invented, it wouldn't matter when since you can travel back in time with the time machine.

9. How many programmers does it take to change a light bulb?
None, because it's a hardware problem.

10. Why did the boy get fired from his keyboard factory job?
He was not doing enough shifts.

11. A chemist walks into a pharmacy and asks the pharmacist, "Do you have any acetylsalicylic acid?"
"You mean aspirin?" asked the pharmacist.
"That's it! I can never remember that word."

12. A physicist, while exiting the theatre after seeing Star Wars, bumped into a fellow physicist. Inspired by the movie, he said to his friend, "May the mass times acceleration be with you."

13. When the astronomy department found out their professor was not getting the Nobel Prize this year, they decided to hold a party for him anyway and give him a constellation prize instead.

14. Why do programmers mix up festivals like Halloween with Christmas? Because 31 OCT = 25 DEC.
Explainer: Octal 31 (which abbreviated looks like October 31st, Halloween) is equal to decimal 25 (which abbreviated looks like December 25th,

Christmas). Decimal and octal are number systems with altered bases.

15. The best thing about a Boolean is that even if you are wrong, you are only off by a bit.
Explainer: A Boolean is a data type which can only have one of two possible values: true and false. A data type just means what type of data is held within something—like a variable. The joke, then, is that if you have a Boolean, the most you can be off is a bit, which would just be 0 or 1.

16. Why did the mother put airbags on the computer?
The computer might crash.

17. Why did the PowerPoint presentation decide to cross the road?
He wanted to get to the other slide.

18. Why did the cat decide to buy a computer for herself?
She liked playing with the mouse.

19. How many Microsoft programmers does it take to change a light bulb?
None, as according to them, darkness is the new standard.

20. I once went to the wedding of two antennas. The wedding itself was alright, but the reception was fantastic.

21. There was once an engineer who built an aircraft made from bubbly chocolate. I think it was called an aero plane.

22. One time some sodium snuck up on water, and the water freaked out.
Talk about overreacting.
Explainer: Sodium metal responds to water by forming a colorless solution of sodium hydroxide and releases hydrogen gas, hence the overreaction.

23. The best method for accelerating a computer is the one that boosts it by 9.8 m/s2.
Explainer: If you are experiencing trouble with a slow computer, the quickest way to accelerate it is to throw it out of the window, and the other option is to drop it from a tall height.

24. A good programmer is someone who always looks both ways before crossing a one-way street.

Explainer: As a programmer, you cannot make assumptions about how things will behave in the program you are developing, hence you have to keep checking everything. The joke refers to the fact that the programmer cannot assume that just because the road is one-way, everyone is going to follow that rule.

25. Why did the astronauts love using computers?
They are into space-bar!

26. They say a thermometer is more intelligent than a graduated cylinder because it has more degrees.

27. The interesting thing about engineering toilet paper is that it's an a-ply-ed science.

28. I am a big fan of the band 1022MB. Though you might not have heard of them because they have not had a gig yet.
Explainer: 1022 megabytes make up 1 gigabyte

29. What did the SQL statement say before entering the restaurant? "May I join you?" Explainer: Structured Query Language (SQL) is a standardized programming language used to achieve relational databases and perform numerous operations on the data in them.

30. What did the programmer say to his coffee? First of all, why is he talking to his coffee?

31. A web developer walks into a restaurant. He immediately leaves in disgust as the restaurant was laid out in tables.

32. Programming is 10% science, 20% ingenuity, and 70% getting the ingenuity to work with the science.

33. A man is smoking a cigarette and blowing smoke rings into the air. His girlfriend becomes irritated with the smoke and says, "Can't you see the warning on the cigarette pack? Smoking is hazardous to your health!" To which the man replies, "I am a programmer. We don't worry about warnings; we only worry about errors."

34. What is the difference between a dog and a marine biologist?
One wags a tail, and the other tags a whale.

35. Did you hear the joke about Sodium hypobromite?
NaBrO
Explainer: The formula for sodium hypobromite is NaBrO

36. Google-Earth gave you the opportunity to go and see anywhere in the world. So what do you do?
You go and look at your house!

37. Why are Helium, Curium, and Barium the medical elements?
If you can't heal-ium or cure-ium, you bury-um.

38. The first computer dates back to Adam and Eve.
It was an Apple with limited memory—just one byte. Then, everything crashed.

39. I can't see an end. I have no control, and I don't think there is an escape. I don't even have a home anymore.

I think it's time for a new keyboard.

40. Whoever stole my copy of Microsoft Office, I will hunt you down and I will make you pay.
You have my Word!

41. If the Silver Surfer and Iron Man team up, they would be alloys.
Explainer: An alloy is a mixture of metals in chemistry. Since silver and Iron are metals, and if the Silver Surfer and Iron Man teamed up, they wouldn't just be allies, they would be alloys as well.

42. The optimist sees the glass half full. The pessimist sees the glass half empty. The chemist sees the glass completely full—half with liquid and half with air.
Explainer: A glass is always full of something, be it a solid, liquid, or gas — unless the whole thing exists in a vacuum and all the atoms are removed.

43. Organic chemistry is difficult.
Those who study it have alkynes of trouble.
Explainer: An alkyne is a type of carbon compound with one carbon-to-carbon triple

bond. They are often used and studied in organic chemistry. It's pronounced "al kine." Hence, alkynes of trouble sounds like all kinds of trouble.

44. Did you hear about the man who got cooled to absolute zero?
He is 0K now.
Explainer: The designation oK represents zero Kelvin. What is Kelvin? It's a temperature scale in which zero is the coldest possible temperature, referred to as absolute zero, where molecules stop moving altogether. A person wouldn't actually be OK if cooled to absolute zero, just for your knowledge. Hence, the joke.

45. Anyone know any jokes about sodium?
Na
Explainer: The periodic table symbol for sodium is Na.

46. I had to make these bad chemistry jokes because all the good ones Argon.
Explainer: Argon is a periodic table element. When said out loud, it sounds like you are gone.

47. Biology is the only science in which multiplication is the same thing as division.
Explainer: In the field of biology, cells increase in number when one cell splits into two.

48. A fellow accidentally ingested some alpha-L-glucose and discovered that he had no ill effect. Apparently he was ambidextrose.
Explainer: Alpha-L-glucose is a low-calorie sweetener alternate for regular D-glucose. Dextrose is a synonym for glucose. Hence, instead of being ambidextrous, the fellow is ambidextrose—meaning he can tolerate either kind of sugar.

49. I want to be something really scary for Halloween this year, so I am dressing up as a phone battery at 2%.

50. Password looks at itself in the mirror. "Don't listen to Google. You are a strong and confident password."

So some of the jokes are definitely complicated for the layman, I hope the explanation helps you understand the actual joke. STEM jokes are best cracked with individuals from the field of STEM. However, easier to understand jokes such as "Smartphones are pacifiers for adults," and "Thanks once again to autocorrect, my sister's kids are expecting the Easter Rabbi tomorrow," can be cracked with everyone. After all, basic technology is understandable by almost everyone.

Jokes aside, STEM is an important field and remember science and facts matter!

In the next chapter, I will share jokes on puns for teenagers.

13

POP'S PUNS FOR THE TEENS

In this chapter of jokes, I am not covering a particular theme per se, but rather an age group which can be hard to please. The jokes are culturally relevant and perhaps more age-appropriate for the stage of life that is most scary for parents—the teen years.

My daughters are 10 and younger, so I have not used these jokes on them. However, I have a nephew and niece in their teens, and I use them as my guinea pigs. Truth be told, sometimes I think they just laugh to keep me happy, after all, I am their uncle!

For a first time dad, the teen years seem a long way away, but you can still start practicing now. The highlight of a dad's life may well be when their teenager turns around and tells them a dad joke. Who knows? Miracles do happen.

The top 50 pop's puns for the teens are:

1. I crashed into McDonald's.
The sign said drive thru!

2. Why does recording a video take so much effort?
You have to use a try-pod.

3. The bakery still owes me money.
Every day I walk in and yell where is my bread!

4. What do you call a muddy motorcycle?
A dirt bike

5. My wife left me after college because I got a bachelor's degree.

6. What is the creepiest part of a car?
A starring wheel

7. Who is the thirstiest cell phone provider?
Tea mobile

8. Gas prices are way too high.
It's $3 per fart.

9. What happens when Thomas Edison doesn't drink water?
He gets light-headed.

10. What did the piano say when it left the house?
I forgot my keys!

11. I accidentally hurt myself in the living room.
I think it's because of the C- ouch!

12. Horses have horseshoes.
I was surprised to see a horse wearing adidas.

13. I drove into an open field and couldn't leave.
All the signs said park.

14. What is a hockey players favorite song?
Ice, ice baby!

15. What do you call a great swimmer?
A dolphin

16. I love spring water.
I can only drink in it in March.

17. What do you call a fly without wings?
A zipper

18. What do directors yell when they get injured?
Cut!

19. What do you call a 60-year-old who has not reached puberty?
A late boomer

20. My high school bully still takes my lunch money.
On the upside, he makes great fries.

21. Were any famous men and women born on your birthday?
No, only babies

22. What is 47 + 11 + 82 + 161 + 99 + 5?
A headache

23. What do pre-teen ducks hate?
Voice quacks

24. What is the difference between the ACT and SAT?
One letter

25. How did the hipster burn his tongue?
He ate the pizza before it was cool.

26. How many Emo kids do you need to screw in a light bulb?
None, they all sit in the dark and cry.

27. A teenager girl had been talking on the phone for 30 minutes and hung up.
Dad: "Wow, that was short! Usually you talk for two hours. What happened?"
She: "Nothing. Just some wrong number."

28. My parents when I was 8: "Go to your room."
My parents now: "Please come out of your room."

29. What does a school and a plant have in common?
STEM

30. What does a high school basketball player and a jury have in common?
The court

31. What book won't teachers give you credit for reading?
Facebook

32. Why did the elephant paint himself different colors?
So he could hide in the crayon box!

33. Why did the gum cross the road?
It was stuck to the chicken's foot!

34. I think my algebra teacher is a pirate.
All she ever wants to do is find X.

35. I sold my vacuum the other day.
All it was doing was collecting dust.

36. Why did the elementary students look up to the high schoolers?
They are smaller, they don't have a choice.

37. Mom: "Hey! Why are you all dressed up? Where are you going?"
Me: "To the bathroom. I need a new Instagram profile picture."

38. What is that thing called when your crush likes you back?
Oh yeah, imagination

39. Those 15-year-old girls talking about "I need a boy who…"
No, you just need to do your homework.

40. Teenager Jamie stormed into the house furiously:
"Dad! You asked me to put a potato in my swimming trunks to impress the girls there!!! You did not specify it had to go in front!!!!!"

41. When my parents are asleep…
Me: "Shhhh…they are sleeping!"
When I am asleep…
Parents: "Let's vacuum the house for 3 hours."

42. "Knock! Knock!"
"Who's there?"
"Yah"
"Yah Who?"
"Naaah bro, I prefer Google."

43. Teacher: "Why are you talking during my lesson?"
Student: "Why are you teaching during my conversation?"

44. Elementary kids have iPhones.
When I was a kid, I put glue on my hands just so I could peel it off when it dried.

45. Teenager—noun: Someone who is ready for the zombie apocalypse but not ready for the math test tomorrow.

46. Teacher: "Where is your homework?"
Me: "I lost it fighting this kid who said you were not the best teacher in school."

47. Phone vibrates at home: You can barely heart it.
Phone vibrates at School: Freaking earthquake!

48. Knock, knock.
Who's there?
Spell.
Spell who?
W-H-O!

Teenage years are hard, and it often feels like kids and parents grow further apart at this age. However your teen might react, enjoy the connection. Teen brains are all over the place, it's like a misled missile—detached at one moment and intense in the next. While dealing with teenagers, you will be as confused as them. Remember, humor, jokes, and interaction really help engage teens. If you want to build a connection with your teen child, then you can use humor to further strengthen and develop that bond.

The limbic system of the brain is an important structure for storing memories. The hippocampus is situated nearby and linked to a structure that aids the production of emotions in the amygdala. This structural relationship guarantees that emotionally charged experiences will be recollected in a better and more efficient way than neutral and every day monotonous events. This serves as a neurological explanation for bringing more emotions (let's hope positive ones) to the classroom. Let's admit it, in today's day and age where all of us have decreased attention spans and very numerous distractions such as our phones, tablets, Netflix, and so on, students need all the help they can get to increase retention of the important information you're teaching them.

ENGAGING TEENS WITH HUMOR

Following are some ways for adding humor to your life along with your teen kids, nephews, nieces, or even teen grandchildren.

One Laugh at a Time

Now, as I have mentioned before, you don't have to be a clown or a standup comedian throwing around jokes every chance you get, even cracking one good joke per day is good enough. Remember, quality over quantity. One of the main tips I would like to give you is that you should say something funny, but relevant as well. Teens are in a different headspace, and their cultural references are on a whole new level, so relevance and humor go hand in hand with them.

It can be anything from a witty one-liner joke to a terrible pun, a hilarious video off YouTube, or a short story of your life. If it fails (do be prepared for silence and rolling eyes in return), laugh about it yourself. At least you tried, and now you have learned what works and what doesn't. Moreover, if you do keep it to one laugh a day, your brain will start to look for humor in everyday life and situation, and you will start feeling creative and lighter.

Use Improv

Have there been moments in your life as a parent, while dealing with teens, when you completely lose them? One second you are talking to them about something important, and the next second you have lost their attention. It's frustrating to say the least. However, what if I told you there is a way around this? You cannot put a stop to their wavering attention, but you can improvise in the moment by using humor, comedy, and animation to make them laugh and bring light to their attention wavering.

Make sure whatever improv you do end up using is relatable. Make sure you convey your feelings about the interruption, so that the audience can relate. This also helps you and your teen kids or relatives to be more in the moment and more mindful of others. Is laughter not a lovely way to inculcate this quality into our teens?

Use the Presence of Friends

During teen years, the opinion of friends and peers matters quite a bit. A series of studies highlighted that teens take more risks in front of their peers. When the teen participants' brains were imaged during risk taking situations and activities, the images showed a rise in blood flow levels in the pleasure center of the brain. This area is a collection of neurons which are activated during the period of gratifying activities.

Hence, when your teen children or relatives are around, try to use humor or involve them in your jokes so there is in increase in interaction. Along with humor, try to include reflective listening and empathy interlaced with humor.

Granted, employing humor in front of teens is difficult. If they sense you are about to crack a joke, even a predictable one, consider the moment ruined. Moreover, keep in mind that their age bracket and their life experience is limited, so mortgage and debt jokes will definitely not work on them. I believe teens work well with short stories, laced with humor, animation, unpredictability, relatability, and pop culture references.

In the next chapter, I will share jokes that are more than one-liners. So, get ready to devote more time to the next chapter.

14

MORE THAN A ONE-LINER

The premise of a dad joke is its brevity and lameness. Technically, this chapter is not about traditional dad jokes since these are longer. However, I thought since you have tried and tested some typical dad jokes, it's now time to get that memory working and try out these amusing longer jokes. Remember, it's all about how you deliver that punchline!

The top 50 more than one-liner jokes are:

1. A woman brings a very limp duck into a veterinary surgeon. As she lays her beloved pet duck on the table, the vet puts his stethoscope to the bird's chest and listens carefully. A moment later, the vet shakes his head and says sadly, "I'm really sorry ma'am, but your

duck, Cuddles, has passed away." The woman becomes quite distressed and begins to cry.

"Are you sure?" she says with tears flooding from her eyes.

"Yes ma'am. I am sure." the vet responds. "Your duck is definitely dead."

"But how can you be so sure?" the woman protests. "I mean, you have not done any testing on him or anything have you? Perhaps he is just stunned or in a coma or something." The vet rolls his eyes then turns around and leaves the room.

A few minutes later, he returns with a black Labrador retriever. As the duck's owner looks on in amazement, the Labrador stands on his hind legs, puts his front paws on the examination table, and sniffs around the duck from top to bottom. He then looks up at the vet with sad eyes and shakes his head. The vet pats the dog on the head and takes it out of the room.

A few minutes later the vet returns with a cat. The cat jumps on the table and delicately sniffs at the bird from its head to its feet. After a moment, the cat looks up, shakes its head, meows softly, and strolls out of the room.

The vet looks at the woman and says, "Look ma'am, I am really sorry, but as I said before, this is most definitely a duck that is no longer of this world. Your duck is dead." The vet then turns to his computer terminal, hits a few keys and produces a bill, which he hands to the woman. The duck's owner, still in shock, looks at the bill and sees it's $150.

"$150 just to tell me my duck is dead!" she shrieks with incredulity.

The vet shrugs his shoulders and says, "I am sorry ma'am. If you had taken my word for it, the bill would have been $20. However, with the lab report and the cat scan, it's now $150."

2. An elderly man had owned his large farm in Louisiana for many years. Right at the back of the farm, there was a large pond ideal for swimming. The old farmer had fixed it up nicely with picnic tables, horseshoe courts, and some apple and peach trees. One evening, the farmer decides to go down to the pond to look it over, as he hadn't been down there for a while. Before setting off, he grabs a five-gallon bucket as he decides he will bring back some fruit.

As he nears the pond, he can hear voices shouting and laughing with glee. Obviously, someone is having a good time. As the farmer gets closer, he can see a bunch of young women who are clearly skinny-dipping in his pond. He makes the women aware of his presence and immediately they all swim over to the far end.

One of the women then shouts, "We are not coming out until you leave mister!"

The farmer replies, "Ladies, I did not come down here to watch you swim naked or make you get out of the pond. You carry on." The wily old-timer then holds up his bucket and says, "I just came down here to feed the alligators!"

Moral of the story: Never underestimate an old man.

3. For a weekend break, three old college buddies go down to Tijuana, Mexico to enjoy a reunion. Well, they had not seen each other for quite a few years, so the stories were long, the laughs were loud, and the booze really did flow that night. They had such a good time, they all woke up the following morning and found themselves in jail. None of them could remember anything. However, within a couple of hours, they are all sentenced to be executed the following day.

The following morning they are all escorted to death row, where Bill, the first of the group is strapped into the electric chair. Bill is asked if he would like to say any words. "Sure," Bill responds. "I am from the Catholic University of America, and I believe in the power of almighty God. I am innocent, and God will intervene."

The executioner throws the switch but nothing happens.

Well, the prison staff can't believe this turn of events. They beg Bill's forgiveness and release him. Next up for the chair is Gary. He is strapped in, and once again, he is offered the opportunity to say something.

"Well, I am from Harvard Law School," says Gary, "and I believe that the power of natural justice will intervene because I am innocent."

Once again, the executioner throws the switch, but nothing happens.

Again the prison staff can't believe this turn of events. They beg Gary's forgiveness and release him.

Finally, Mike is strapped into the chair, and once again he is offered the opportunity to say something.

"Well," says Mike. "I have a PhD in electrical engineering from the Massachusetts Institute of Technology and I can tell you now, you won't be executing anyone if you don't plug this thing in."

4. Jack is a cowboy working on a large ranch in a remote pasture in Wyoming. One day, as he is overseeing the livestock on the ranch, a brand-new 7 Series BMW suddenly advances towards him creating an enormous cloud of dust in the process.

The car stops and the driver is a young man in a Brioni suit, Gucci shoes, Ray-Ban sunglasses, and YSL tie. He steps out of the car and says to the cowboy, "If I tell you exactly how many cows and calves you have in your herd, will you give me a calf?"

Jack looks at the man, who is obviously a yuppie, he then looks at his peacefully grazing animals and responds calmly, "Sure, why not?"

The yuppie then whips out a very impressive iPhone 13 Pro smartphone from his jacket pocket and begins to surf the NASA website. Simultaneously he uses the GPS satellite to get the exact coordinates of his location. He then feeds that back to Google Earth to capture a high-resolution image of this location.

The young man then opens the digital image in Photoshop and exports it to an image processing facility in Langley, Virginia.

Within seconds, he receives an email to his iPhone 13 Pro to confirm that the image has been processed and the data captured and stored. He then accesses an MS-

SQL database through an ODBC connected Excel spreadsheet and, after a few minutes, receives a response.

Finally, he uses an AirPrint printer located in his car to print out a full-color, 150-page report. He then turns to Jack, hands him the report and says, "Sir, you will see from the Executive Summary that you have exactly 1,586 cows and calves."

"That is right," says Jack. "I guess you can take one of my calves."

Jack then watches with amusement as the young man struggles to get the animal into the trunk of his car.

After a minute or two, Jack says to the guy, "Hey, if I can tell you exactly what your business is, will you give me my calf back?"

The young man thinks for a second and then he says, "Sure, why not?"

"You're a Congressman for the US Government," says Jack.

"Wow! That is correct," says the yuppie, "but how did you guess that?"

"No guessing required son," Jack responded. "You showed up here even though nobody called you; you want paying for an answer I already know; to a question, I never asked. You used millions of dollars' worth of equipment trying to show me how smart you are; and you don't know a thing about how ordinary, working people make a living, or about cows for that matter. If you did, you would know that this herd is actually a flock of sheep. Now give me back my dog."

5. An old Native American man needs to borrow $500, so he goes to his local bank and asks to speak with the Loans Officer. The banker welcomes him and then says a loan application form must be completed. So he takes a loan application form from his desk drawer and begins to question the old man.

"So, what are you going to do with the money?" he asks the man.

"Buy silver, make jewelry, then sell it," the man responded.

"What have you got for collateral?" asked the banker.

"I don't know collateral," replied the old man.

"Well, that is something of value that you provide us with to cover the cost of the loan if you fail to repay," said the banker. "For instance, have you got any vehicles?"

"Yes. I have a 1979 Chevy pickup," replied the old man.

The banker shook his head, "No that will not do, I am afraid. How about livestock?"

"Yes, I have a horse," replied the old man.

"How old is it?" the banker inquired.

"I don't know, it has no teeth," replies the old man.

The conversation went on like this for a while but eventually, the banker decides to grant the $500 loan to the old man. Several weeks later the old man returns to the bank.

He pulls out a large roll of $100 bills from his pocket, "I am here to pay," he says.

He then hands the banker $500 in $100 bills to repay his loan.

"Business has been good I can see," says the banker. "What are you going to do with the rest of that money?"

"Keep it close to me," the old man responded.

"Why don't you just deposit it in my bank?" the banker inquired.

"I don't know what deposit is," replied the old man.

"Well, you just put the money in our bank, and we take care of it for you. Whenever you want to use it, you can withdraw it," the banker responded.

The old Native American man leans across the desk and looks the banker in the eye and asks, "What have you got for collateral?"

6. A man is dining alone in a fancy restaurant, and there is a beautiful redhead sitting at the next table. He has been sneakily checking her out ever since he arrived, but doesn't have the courage to start talking to her.

Suddenly she sneezes and her glass eye comes flying out of its socket toward the man. His reflexes kick in and he reaches out, plucks it out of the air, and hands it back to her.

The redhead is mortified. "Oh my, I am so sorry," she says as she pops her eye back into place. "Let me buy your dinner to make it up to you."

So, he joins her table, and they enjoy a wonderful meal together. Afterwards, they go to the theatre followed by drinks at a bar. They talk, they laugh, she shares her deepest dreams, and he shares his. She listens.

After paying for everything, she asks him if he would like to come to her place for a nightcap. He says yes, and they return to her place.

He ends up staying the night. The next morning, she cooks a gourmet meal with all the trimmings. The guy is amazed at how everything has been so perfect and how incredible this woman is. He can't believe his luck. "You know," he said, "you are the perfect woman, are you this nice to every guy you meet?"

"No," she replies, "You just happened to catch my eye."

7. Two men are walking through the woods one day when they stumble across a big, deep hole. The first man peers into it and says, "Wow! That looks deep." The second man says, "It sure does. Let's throw a few pebbles in there and see how deep it is. We will be able to tell the depth by how long it is before we hear the noise of the pebbles landing."

So they pick up a few pebbles and throw them in and wait. Nothing. There is no noise. The first guy says, "Jeeez. That is really deep. I know, let's throw one of these great big rocks down there. Those should make a noise."

So they pick up a couple football-sized rocks and toss them into the hole and wait... and wait... Again, nothing.

They look at each other in amazement. Then the first man gets a determined look on his face and says, "Hey, over here in the weeds, there is a railroad tie. Help me carry it over. When we toss that sucker in, it has got to make some noise." So, the two of them drag the heavy tie over to the hole and heave it in. Once again, not a sound comes from the hole.

Suddenly, out of the nearby woods, a goat appears, running like the wind. It rushes toward the two men, then right past them, running as fast as its legs will carry it. Suddenly it leaps in the air and into the hole. The two men are astonished with what they have just seen and look at each other in amazement.

Then, out of the woods comes a farmer who spots the men and ambles over. He asks them, "Hey, you two guys seen my goat out here?"

The first man says, "You bet we did! Craziest thing I ever saw. It came running like crazy and just jumped into this hole and disappeared!"

"Nah", says the farmer, "That couldn't have been my goat. My goat was chained to a railroad tie."

8. A husband and wife who work for the circus go to an adoption agency looking to adopt a child, but the social workers there raise doubts about their suitability. So, the couple produce photos of their 50-foot motor

home, which is clean and well maintained and equipped with a beautiful nursery. The social workers are satisfied by this but then raise concerns about the kind of education a child would receive while in the couple's care.

The husband puts their mind at ease, saying, "We have arranged for a full-time tutor who will teach the child all the usual subjects along with French, Mandarin, and computer skills." Next though, the social workers express concern about a child being raised in a circus environment. This time the wife explains, "Our nanny is a certified expert in pediatric care, welfare, and diet."

The social workers are finally satisfied and ask the couple, "What age child are you hoping to adopt?" The husband says, "It doesn't really matter, as long as the kid fits in the cannon."

9. A New York attorney representing a wealthy art collector called his client and said to him, "Saul, I have some good news and I have some bad news."

The art collector replied, "I have had an awful day; let's hear the good news first."

The attorney said, "Well, I met with your wife today, and she informed me that she invested $5,000 in two pictures that she thinks will bring a minimum of $15-20 million. I think she could be right."

Saul replied enthusiastically, "Well done! My wife is a brilliant businesswoman! You have just made my day. Now I know I can handle the bad news. What is it?"

The attorney replied, "The pictures are of you with your secretary."

10. A young man named Tommy bought a horse from a farmer for $250, and the farmer agreed to deliver the horse to Tommy the following day.

The next day though, the farmer turned up at Tommy's house and said, "Sorry son, but I have some bad news, the horse died."

Tommy replied, "Well, then just give me my money back. That is fine."

The farmer said, "Sorry, I can't do that. I went and spent it already."

Tommy then said, "Okay, then, just bring me the dead horse."

The farmer was surprised and asked Tommy, "Why? What are you going to do with him?"

Tommy replied, "I am going to raffle him off."

The farmer laughed and said, "You can't raffle off a dead horse! Who would buy a ticket?"

Tommy answered, "Sure I can, just watch me. I just won't tell anybody the horse is dead."

A month later, the farmer met up with Tommy again and asked, "What happened with that dead horse in the end. Did you raffle him off?"

Tommy said, "I sure did. I sold 500 tickets at $5 a piece."

The farmer said, "Did anyone complain?"

Tommy smiled and said, "Just the guy who won. So I gave him his $5 back."

11. A multi-millionaire living in Darwin, Australia, decided to throw a party and invited all of his buddies and neighbors. He also invited Brian, the only Aborigine in the neighborhood. He held the party around the pool in the backyard of his mansion. Everyone was having a good time drinking, dancing, eating prawns and oysters from the barbecue, and flirting.

Then, at the height of the party, the millionaire said, "I have a 15 foot man-eating crocodile in my pool, and I will give a million dollars to anyone who will join him in the pool." The words were barely out of his mouth when there was a loud splash.

Everyone turned around and saw Brian in the pool fighting madly with the crocodile, jabbing it in the eyes with his thumbs, throwing punches, head butting it, getting it in choke holds, biting its tail and flipping it through the air like some kind of martial arts expert.

The water was churning and splashing everywhere. Both Brian and the crocodile were screaming and raising hell. Finally, after what seemed like an age, Brian strangled the crocodile and let it float to the top of the pool like a dead goldfish.

An exhausted Brian wearily climbed out of the pool with everybody staring at him in disbelief.

The millionaire said, "Well, Brian, I reckon I owe you a million dollars then."

"Nah, you all right boss, I don't want it," said Brian.

So, the millionaire said, "Man, I have to give you something. You won the bet. How about half a million bucks?"

"No thanks, I don't want it," Brian insisted.

The millionaire said, "Come on, I insist on giving you something. That was amazing. How about a new Porsche, a Rolex, and some stock options?"

Once again, Brian said, "No."

Confused, the rich man asked, "Well Brian, then what do you want?"

"I want the bastard who pushed me in," said Brian.

12. These three guys die together in a tragic accident and they all go to heaven.

When they get there, St. Peter greets them and tells them, "We only have one rule here in heaven. Don't step on the ducks."

So, they enter heaven and sure enough, there are ducks all over the place.

It's almost impossible not to step on a duck because there are so many, and though they try their utmost to avoid standing on them, the first guy soon accidentally steps on one.

St. Peter then appears with the ugliest woman the guy had ever seen.

St. Peter chains the woman to the guy and says to him, "Your punishment for stepping on a duck is to spend eternity chained to this ugly woman!"

The next day, the second guy also accidentally steps on a duck. Once again, St. Peter shows up and with him is another extremely ugly woman. He chains the woman to the second guy saying, "Your punishment for stepping on a duck is to spend eternity chained to this ugly woman!"

The third guy has observed all this, and as he really doesn't want to be chained to an ugly woman for eternity, he is extremely careful where he steps.

Indeed, he manages to go months without stepping on any ducks. One day though, St. Peter appears with the most gorgeous woman the guy has ever laid eyes on. She is tall, curvaceous, tanned, and extremely sexy.

Without a word, St. Peter chains the woman to the third guy.

The guy happily says to the woman, "I wonder what I did to deserve being chained to you for all eternity?"

The woman replies, "I don't know about you, but I stepped on a duck."

13. A father was walking past his son's bedroom one day and happened to look in.

He was astonished to see that his bed was nicely made, and everything was picked up off the floor. Then he saw an envelope, propped up prominently on the pillow that was addressed to "Dad."

Fearing the worst, he opened the envelope with trembling hands and read the letter. It said:

Dear Dad,

It's with great regret and sadness that I am writing to you. I had to elope with my new girlfriend because I wanted to avoid a scene with you and Mom.

I have been finding real passion with Susie, and she is so nice. I knew you wouldn't approve of her because of all her piercings, tattoos, tight motorcycle clothes, and the fact that she is much older than I am.

It's not only the passion. Dad, she is pregnant.

Don't worry though. Susie said that we will be very happy. She owns a trailer in the woods and has a stack of firewood for the whole winter. We share a dream of having many more children.

Susie has also opened my eyes to the fact that marijuana doesn't really hurt anyone. We will be growing it for ourselves and trading it with the other people that live nearby for cocaine and ecstasy.

In the meantime, we will pray that science finds a cure for AIDS, so that Susie can get better. She deserves it.

Don't worry Dad. I am 15, and I know how to take care of myself.

Someday I am sure that we will be back to visit, so that you can get to know your grandchildren.

Love, Your son Tim.

P.S. Dad, none of the above is true. I am over at Jimmy's house. I just wanted to remind you that there are worse things in life than a lousy report card.

It's in my desk drawer.

I love you.

14. When NASA was preparing for the Apollo project, they did some astronaut training on a Navajo Indian reservation.

One day, a Navajo elder and his son were herding sheep and came across the space crew. The old man, who only spoke Navajo, asked a question, which the son translated, "What are the guys in the big suits doing?"

A member of the crew said they were practicing for their trip to the moon. The old man got really excited, and asked if he could send a message to the moon with the astronauts.

Recognizing a promotional opportunity for the spin-doctors, the NASA folks found a tape recorder.

After the old man recorded his message, they asked the son to translate. He refused. So the NASA reps brought the tape to the reservation, where the rest of the tribe listened and laughed, but refused to translate the elder's message to the moon.

Finally, NASA called in an official government translator. He reported that the moon message said, "Watch out for these guys; they have come to steal your land."

15. It's the World Cup Final, and a man makes his way to his seat right next to the pitch. He sits down, noticing that the seat next to him is empty. He leans over and asks his neighbor if someone will be sitting there. "No," says the neighbor.

"The seat is empty. This is incredible," said the man. "Who in their right mind would have a seat like this for the Final and not use it?"

The neighbor says, "Well, actually the seat belongs to me. I was supposed to come with my wife, but she passed away. This is the first World Cup Final we have not been to together since we got married."

"Oh, I'm so sorry to hear that. That is terrible. Could you not find someone else—a friend, relative, or even a neighbor to take her seat?"

The man shakes his head. "No," he says. "They're all at the funeral."

16. Sid and Irv are business partners. They make a deal that whichever one dies first will contact the living one from the afterlife. So, Irv dies. Sid doesn't hear from him for about a year and figures there is no afterlife. Then one day he gets a call. It's Irv. "So there is an afterlife! What is it like?" Sid asks.

"Well, I sleep very late. I get up and have a big breakfast. Then, I have sex—lots of sex. Then, I go back to sleep, but I get up for lunch. I have a big lunch, have some more sex, and take a nap. I have a huge dinner and more sex. I go to sleep and wake up the next day."

"Oh, my God," says Sid. "So that is what heaven is like?"

"Oh no," says Irv. "I am not in heaven. I am a bear in Yellowstone Park."

17. A man dies and is sent to hell. Satan meets him, shows him doors to three rooms, and says he must choose one to spend eternity in. In the first room, people are standing in dirt up to their necks. The man says, "No, let me see the next room." In the second room, people are standing in dirt up to their noses. The man says no again. Finally Satan opens the third room. People are standing with dirt up to their knees, drinking coffee and eating pastries. The man says, "I pick this room."

Satan says, "Ok" and starts to leave, and the guy wades in and starts pouring some coffee. On the way out, Satan yells, "OK, coffee break is over. Everyone back on your heads!"

18. A young boy enters a barber shop, and the barber whispers to his customer. "This is the dumbest kid in the world. Watch while I prove it you." The barber puts a dollar bill in one hand and two quarters in the other, then calls the boy over and asks, "Which do you want, son?" The boy takes the quarters and leaves. "What did I tell you?" said the barber. "That kid never learns!" Later, when the customer leaves, he sees the same young boy coming out of the ice cream store.

"Hey, son! May I ask you a question? Why did you take the quarters instead of the dollar bill?"

The boy licked his cone and replied, "Because the day I take the dollar, the game is over!"

19. A man and his wife are at a restaurant, and the husband keeps staring at an old drunken lady swigging her gin at a nearby table. His wife asks, "Do you know her?"

"Yes," sighs the husband. "She is my ex-wife. She took to drinking right after we divorced seven years ago, and I hear she has not been sober since."

"My God!" says the wife. "Who would think a person could go on celebrating that long?"

20. A tough old cowboy from Texas counseled his granddaughter that if she wanted to live a long life, the secret was to sprinkle a pinch of gun powder on her oatmeal every morning.

The granddaughter did this religiously until the age of 103, when she died.

She left behind 14 children, 30 grandchildren, 45 great-grandchildren, 25 great-great-grandchildren, and a 40-foot hole where the crematorium used to be.

21. My friend once called a few house painters to his house for some work. He wanted them to paint his porch. After a few hours, the house painters came back for the payment as their work was complete. Before leaving, they told my friend that they had enjoyed painting his car, but it's not really a Porsche.

22. There is a skeleton in our neighborhood who always knows that something bad might happen way before it actually happens. He has actually become quite famous and when a TV crew interviewed him about the reason behind this ability, the skeleton finally disclosed his secret: he could feel the bad vibes in his bones.

23. I visited a cafe one day with my friends. The waiter recommended that we try their special coffee. We agreed and soon the coffee arrived. As we drank the coffee, we realized that it tasted like dirt and mud. Disgusted by the fact, all of us complained immediately.

The alarmed waiter rushes over and says, "Well Sir, it was freshly ground coffee!"

24. A family was having dinner once when the youngest boy asked his father whether worms tasted nice when we eat them. Both the parents reprimanded the little boy and told him that these things should not be discussed over the dinner table. When the father asked the boy after dinner why he had asked such a question, he replied, "Papa, I think worms taste okay because there was one in your noodles."

25. After Sunday church, the priest would hand us each an orange and a big cookie. A little girl once lied and took two oranges, but the priest told her she must not lie because God is watching. Then, the girl took two cookies and lied about it. When asked why she had done that, she said because she thought that God was only watching oranges.

26. Once during an adventure, a farmer named Bryan Clay stumbled into a cave and found a magic lamp. Upon rubbing the lamp, a Genie appeared and asked him what his wish was. The farmer told him that he

wished he were very rich. The Genie said okay and asked him, "Alright Mr. Very Rich Clay, what is your second wish?"

27. I went to this haunted house for exploration. It was near the forest, so the local guide warned me that I might find some animals there. Sure enough, there was a panda. When I offered it some food, I was taken aback because it suddenly started talking. Turned out that it was a ghost panda, and it only ate bam-booooo!

28. As a group of robbers entered the bank, their leader went to the manager and asked him to open the vault. He threatened the manager by saying, "If you try to do anything smart, you are fiction."

The manager was confused and asked him, "Do you not mean 'You are history?'"

The robber angrily replied back, "Don't change the subject, okay?"

29. I was in the library once when a man walked in asking for some ham and cheese. The librarian politely told him that he was in a library. The man first apolo-

gized and then whispered to the librarian, "Can I please have some ham and cheese?"

30. I was in my garden when I got the news that my father had fallen from a 20 feet ladder and was in the hospital. I rushed to the hospital expecting that my father had some major fractures, but he was alright except for some minor cuts. When I told him that it was a miracle, he disagreed and told me, "Son, I had just fallen from the first step of the ladder."

31. After a prolonged drought, when the rain came, all the animals in the forest were happy except the Kangaroo. When the others asked him what the reason was for such sadness, the Kangaroo revealed that the rain meant that all its kids would now be playing inside.

32. I was visiting the house of a distant cousin when I saw that he was playing chess with his cat. I said that it had to be the most intelligent cat ever. My cousin replied, "Absolutely not! She has lost all her matches!"

33. My brother came back from school all motivated because he said he would be following a new diet from that day forward. We did not really give it much thought until my brother started eating his homework for dinner. When we stopped him and asked why he was doing that, he replied, "I was just trying to see how it tasted because my teacher said that the homework would be a piece of cake for me."

34. In my neighborhood, there was a couple who had given their twin sons very weird names. One was named Trouble, while the other boy's name was Mind Your Own Business. So, one day they were playing hide and seek. Mind Your Own Business counted to a hundred and then started looking for his brother. But, somehow he couldn't find him anywhere. He saw a police car passing the neighborhood, so he stopped it to ask for help. When the police officer asked him for his name, he replied, "Mind Your Own Business!" Feeling insulted, the police officer still asked politely who he was looking for. Mind Your Own Business replied, "I am looking for Trouble!"

35. The historians had gathered for a party in Cairo after they had discovered a new mummy. The discov-

ered mummy, on display at the party hall, suddenly woke up. Seeing the historians alarmed, the mummy said that he just wanted to listen to some music. The mummy said, "Please don't play jazz because my trombones are in a very bad shape. Could someone please put on some wrap music?"

36. A food critic visits a local restaurant to review its food for the town magazine. The owner welcomes him and shows him to the table. The food is presented to him, and after a while, the critic calls the owner to say that there is something missing in his bowl of soup. The owner asks whether it's too spicy or sweet or salty. When the food critic says no, the owner decides to taste the soup himself but he cannot find the spoon. "Yeah," says the critic, "that is what is missing."

37. I was once passing through a town in England when this lady stopped me because she needed help fixing her car that had broken down. As I was fixing the car, the lady would cross the road and shout "Hello" at me. This happened a few times as the lady found it really amusing. I would have thought that it was very weird had I not realized that it was the singer Adele.

38. For a high school dance, the head boy asked out the girl he liked. To get flowers for her, he had to stand in a line outside the florist for an hour. To make things worse, he had to wait another hour in a line outside the tuxedo shop. Finally, he goes to the dance with the girl. The girl wanted to have some apple punch, so the boy went to get it, but to his surprise, there was no punch line.

39. I was in a barbershop when a man and his young son walked in to get a haircut. The man asked the barber to give his son a haircut while he shopped for groceries nearby. The barber finished giving the haircut, but there was no sign of the father. An hour passed; two hours passed. He finally asked the son where his father was. The boy shocked us by saying, "That man was not my father. He just told me that if I wanted to get a free haircut at the barbershop, I should come with him."

40. Once, a mosquito walked into a clinic. The doctor saw him and asked him what the matter was. The mosquito said that he had a lot of problems. He was not happy with his life and he was not happy with the job he was doing. He was sad and had no motivation. The

doctor listened to his problems and told him that he should really visit a therapist instead of a doctor. The mosquito replied, "Yeah, I know. I just came in because of the blood."

41. Britain's oldest woman turned 114 today. When asked the secret of her longevity, she attributed it to taking a walk at midnight every night. When quizzed on whether she was concerned about the increase in muggings in recent years, she said that she was not and would continue mugging people as long as her health holds out.

42. The blonde's password: During a recent password audit, it was found that a blonde was using the following password: "MickeyMinniePlutoHueyLouie-DeweyDonaldGoofySacramento."

When asked why such a long password, she said she was told that it had to be at least 8 characters long and include at least one capital.

43. An eight-year old boy had never spoken a word. One afternoon, as he sat eating his lunch, he turned to his mother and said, "The soup is cold."

His astonished mother exclaimed, "Son, I have waited so long to hear you speak, but all these years you never said a thing. Why have you not spoken before?"

The boy looked at her and replied, "Up until now, everything has been satisfactory."

44. After being unhappy for many years, my mother came to me and said she was going to get a sex change operation. I did not fully understand, but I was very supportive throughout the whole operation, then he came home.

That is when it all started—all the time, all day long, horrible dad jokes, terrible puns, and all around just awful humor. After a few weeks and being fed up, I realized something and I confronted them.

"Did you seriously have a sex change operation just for the dad jokes?!" I asked.

He replied, "Oh, you could see right through me, I must be so trans-parent."

45. A man takes his wife to get tested. Several days go by, and he receives a call from the doctor. The doctor tells him, "Due to an unfortunate mix up with the lab,

we are not sure if your wife has Covid-19 or Alzheimer's."

The man, clearly frustrated, asks, "Well, what am I supposed to do with that kind of information?"

The doctor calmly suggests, "I recommend you take her for a very long walk and leave her. If she comes home, don't let her in."

46. I was in a long McDonalds drive-through line this morning, and the young lady behind me leaned on her horn because I was taking too long to place my order.

Take the high road, I thought to myself. So, when I got to the first window I paid for her order along with my own.

The cashier must have told her what I had done because as we moved up she leaned out her window and waved to me and mouthed, "Thank you," obviously embarrassed that I had repaid her rudeness with kindness.

When I got to the second window, I showed them both receipts and took her food too.

Now she has to go back to the end of the line to start all over.

47. A fellow was walking along a country road when he came upon a farmer working in his field. The man called out to the farmer, "How long will it take me to get to the next town?"

The farmer did not answer. The man waited a bit and then started walking again. After the man had gone about a hundred yards, the farmer yelled out, "About 20 minutes."

"Thank you, but why did you not tell me that when I asked you?"

"I did not know how fast you could walk."

48. Tim decided to tie the knot with his long-time girlfriend. One evening, after the honeymoon, he was organizing his golfing equipment. His wife was standing nearby watching him.

After a long period of silence, she finally spoke, "Tim, I have been thinking, now that we are married maybe it's time you quit golfing. You spend so much time on the course. You could probably get a good price for your clubs."

Tim got this horrified look on his face.

She says, "Darling, what is wrong?"

"For a minute there you were beginning to sound like my ex-wife."

"Ex-wife!" she screams. "I did not know you were married before!"

"I was not," he replied.

49. A woman asked an Army General when the last time he had made love to a woman. The general replied, "1956, ma'am."

The woman in disbelief said "1956?! That long? Come with me, and let me make your night better." The woman and general went back to her apartment and made passionate love for over an hour. Afterwards, the woman cuddled up to the general and said "Well, you sure have not forgotten anything since 1956..."

The general looked at her, confused, and replied "I sure hope not, it's only 2130 now."

50. Donald Trump was walking through Manhattan and saw a long line. Wondering what it was for, he joined it. People would look over their shoulder, see that is was Donald Trump behind them, and leave the line, so he would proceed closer and closer to the front.

As he was getting closer to the head of the line, he asked one man, who also looked and was about to walk away, "Wait a second, what is this line for and why are you now leaving it?"

The man said, "This is the line for Canadian Immigration Visas, but if you are getting one, I don't need one now."

As a bonus, since I want to spread laughter and happiness in abundance, I am going to add five more long jokes! Lucky you.

Here goes:

1. So there was this man in Bulgaria who drove trains for a living. He loved his job. Driving a train had been his dream ever since he was a child. He loved to make the train go as fast as possible. Unfortunately, one day he was a little too reckless and caused a crash. He made it out, but a single person died. Well, needless to say, he went to court over this incident. He was found guilty and was sentenced to death by electrocution. When the day of the execution came, he requested a single banana as his last meal. After eating the banana, he was strapped into the electric chair. The switch was flown, sparks flew, and smoke filled the air, but nothing happened. The man was perfectly fine.

Well, at the time, there was an old Bulgarian law that said a failed execution was a sign of divine intervention, so the man was allowed to go free. Somehow, he managed to get his old job back driving the train. Having not learned his lesson at all, he went right back to driving the train with reckless abandon. Once again, he caused a train to crash, this time killing two people. The trial went much the same as the first, resulting in a sentence of execution. For his final meal, the man requested two bananas. After eating the bananas, he was strapped into the electric chair. The switch was thrown, sparks flew, smoke filled the room, and the man was once again unharmed.

Well, this of course meant that he was free to go. Once again, he somehow managed to get his old job back. To what should have been the surprise of no one, he crashed yet another train and killed three people. So, he once again found himself being sentenced to death. On the day of his execution, he requested his final meal: three bananas.

"You know what? No," said the executioner. "I have had it with you and your stupid bananas and walking out of here unharmed. I am not giving you a thing to eat; we are strapping you in and doing this now." Well, it was against protocol, but the man was strapped in to the electric chair without a last meal. The switch was pulled, sparks flew, smoke filled the room, and the man was still unharmed. The executioner was speechless. The man looked at the executioner and said, "Oh, the bananas had nothing to do with it. I am just a bad conductor."

2. One day, Einstein has to speak at an important science conference.

On the way there, he tells his driver that looks a bit like him,

"I am sick of all these conferences. I always say the same things over and over!"

The driver agrees, "You are right. As your driver, I attended all of them, and even though I don't know anything about science, I could give the conference in your place."

"That is a great idea!" says Einstein. "Let's switch places then!"

So, they switch clothes, and as soon as they arrive, the driver dressed as Einstein goes on stage and starts giving the usual speech, while the real Einstein, dressed as the car driver, attends it.

However, in the crowd there is one scientist who wants to impress everyone and thinks of a very difficult question to ask Einstein, hoping he will not be able to respond. This guy stands up and interrupts the conference by posing his very difficult question. The whole room goes silent, holding their breath, waiting for the response.

The driver looks at him, dead in the eye, and says,

"Sir, your question is so easy to answer that I am going to let my driver reply to it for me."

3. So, the Pope is super early for his flight. He asks his driver on the way to the airport if he could drive around for a while because they have time to kill and he has not driven a car since becoming the Pope.

Naturally, he is a bit rusty, so he is driving poorly, when suddenly he sees police lights behind him. He pulls over, and when the officer comes up to the window his eyes go wide. He says to the Pope, "Hold on for a minute," and goes back to his car to radio the chief.

Cop: "Chief we have a situation. I have pulled over an important figure."

Chief: "How important? A governor or something?"

Cop: "No sir. He is bigger."

Chief: "So, what? A celebrity or something?"

Cop: "More important, sir."

Chief: "A major politician?"

Cop: "No sir, he is much more important."

Chief: "Well, who is it!?"

Cop: "Well, actually I am not sure, but the Pope is his driver."

4. Three couples are trying to get married at the same church. There is a young couple, a middle-aged couple, and an elderly couple. The three couples meet with the priest and discuss when they can get married.

"If you wish to get married in my church, you must all go one month without having sex," says the priest. One month later the three couples return to the church and talk to the priest.

He then asks the elderly couple, "Have you completed the month without sex?"

"Yes we have, it was easy," replies the elderly couple.

"How about you?" he asks the middle-aged couple.

"It was hard, but we did not have sex for the whole month," they respond.

"How about you two?" he asks the young couple.

"No, we couldn't do it," responds the boyfriend.

"Tell me why," says the priest.

"Well, my girlfriend had a can of corn in her hand, and she accidentally dropped it. She bent over to pick it up, and that is when it happened."

The priest then tells them, "You are not welcome in my church."

"We are not welcome in the supermarket either," says the boyfriend.

5. In World War I, there was trench warfare, and neither the Americans nor the Germans could get the upper hand. They were reaching a stalemate. One day, an American came up with a plan that would win them the war. This private explained his plan to his trench mates, and they figured, "Why not? It's not like we have any better ideas."

The next day, an American soldier called out, "Hans!?"

A German popped up and shouted back, "Ja?!" Boom, the German was shot dead. The next day the Americans shouted again, "Hans?!"

"Ja?!" Shot dead. This process continued over the next couple of days. The Germans were losing large numbers and were now finally catching on.

The Germans had an emergency meeting. They thought they could come back from the heavy losses using the same tactics as the Americans. Thus, a German asked, "What is a popular American name?"

"John!" replied another. The next day, the Germans decided to execute their plan.

A German shouted, "John!?"

An American called back, "Is that you Hans?!"

"Ja!"

That is how the Americans won World War I.

I hope you enjoyed these longer jokes. While they may be tougher to recall and relate, you can always enjoy them for your own entertainment and have a good laugh by yourself.

However, due to the fact that I have told some jokes repeatedly over a period of time, I know them by heart and am able to crack the longer jokes whenever the situation arises. For instance, I have told the Donald Trump one numerous times during the tenure of his presidency, and it received a lot of laughter. So, pick a few you like and learn them by heart. It seems a bit daunting, but it's not!

Admittedly, I don't crack the longer jokes with my children. I feel one-liners work best on their age group since their attention is easily distracted, and they will begin to think your jokes are boring. The last thing I want is for my daughters to think I am boring.

In the next chapter, I will be sharing the best of the best dad jokes.

15

THE BEST OF THE BEST

As we near the end of the book, I want to share the best of the best jokes out there with you. I will cover longer and shorter jokes so that you may share them with any age group you want; the more the merrier, right? I know the best jokes are subjective, but I hope you trust my humor enough by now and can be assured that I will actually share the best funny jokes!

The top 50 best of the best jokes are:

1. What do you call a zombie who cooks stir fries?
Dead man wok-ing

2. Why did the scarecrow get an award?
He was out standing in his field!

3. I was stood behind a customer at an ATM, and he turned around and said "could you check my balance?" So, I pushed him.

His balance was not that great.

4. I was wondering why the frisbee kept looking bigger and bigger, and then it hit me.

5. I have a fear of speed bumps.

I am slowly getting over it.

6. I have a fear of elevators, but I have started taking steps to avoid it.

7. I was addicted to soap, but I am clean now.

8. If you see a crime at an Apple store, are you an iWitness?

9. If the early bird catches the worm, I will sleep in until there are pancakes.

10. The wedding was so beautiful, even the cake was in tiers.

11. Did you know that milk is the fastest liquid on earth?
It's pasteurized before you can even see it.

12. Why are spiders so smart?
They can find everything on the web.

13. How do lawyers say goodbye?
We will be suing ya!

14. Wanna hear a joke about paper?
Never mind—it's tearable.

15. Every time I take my dog to the park, the ducks try to bite him.
That is what I get for buying a pure bread dog.

16. Which is faster, hot or cold?
Hot, because you can catch a cold.

17. Why is cold water so insecure?
It's never called hot.

18. Why is it bad to iron your four-leaf clover?
You should not press your luck.

19. What rock group has four men who don't sing?
Mount Rushmore

20. What do you call it when Batman skips church?
Christian Bale

21. Did you hear about the man who fell into an upholstery machine?
He is fully recovered now.

22. Why are elevator jokes so good?
They work on so many levels.

23. Do you know the story about the chicken that crossed the border?
Me neither, I couldn't follow it.

24. How can a leopard change his spots?
By moving

25. What did the zero say to the eight?
That belt looks good on you.

26. I got carded at a liquor store, and my Blockbuster card accidentally fell out. The cashier said, "never mind."

27. When I was a kid, my mother told me I could be anyone I wanted to be.
Turns out, identity theft is a crime.

28. What did the police officer say to his bellybutton?
You are under a vest.

29. What do you call it when a group of apes starts a company?
Monkey business

30. My wife asked me to stop singing *Wonderwall* to her.
I said maybe…

31. Want to know why nurses like red crayons? Sometimes they have to draw blood.

32. My wife asked me to go get 6 cans of Sprite from the grocery store.
I realized when I got home that I had picked 7 up.

33. Why were the utensils stuck together?
They were spooning.

34. I was going to tell a time-traveling joke, but you guys did not like it.

35. Shouldn't the "roof" of your mouth actually be called the ceiling?

36. Stop looking for the perfect match…use a lighter.

37. I told my doctor I heard buzzing, but he said it's just a bug going around.

38. Why was the dad sitting on a pack of playing cards?
His kid asked him to sit on the deck.

39. How did the dad prank his daughter using fake dog poop on April Fools Day? He told her to look out for her new sham-poo in the shower.

40. What was said about the messy, angry man who was eating a can of Pringles? "He's got a chip on his shoulder."

41. My wife and I let astrology get between us.
It Taurus apart.

42. What do you call a coupon-using vampire?
Suckers for deals

43. Why do standup comedians perform poorly in Hawaii?
The audience only responds in a low ha.

44. I was in a grocery store when a man started to throw cheese, butter and yoghurt at me.
How Dairy!

45. I had a fun childhood. My dad used to push me down the hill in old tires.
They were Goodyears.

46. My son knocked a picture of himself off the shelf. He looked devastated.
I told him, "Don't worry about it, champ. Pick yourself up."

47. I told my wife that a husband is like a fine wine; we just get better with age. The next day, she locked me in the cellar.

48. Did you hear about the new restaurant called Karma?
There is no menu—you get what you deserve.

49. What is the difference between a poorly dressed man on a unicycle and a well-dressed man on a bicycle?
Attire

50. What do you need to make a small fortune on Wall Street?
A large fortune

My all-time favorite is, "Why are spiders so smart? They can find everything on the web." While the web is a very archaic term, especially for children, I still find it funny. I have cracked it numerous times. I know this is the one joke to which my daughters will always respond to with, "ugh dad, this is the worst joke ever." It is then that I know, I have succeeded at being the king of dad jokes!

THAT'S A WRAP, FOLKS!

Now folks, we have come to the end of this hilarious journey. I hope all of you had your fair share of laughter, giggles, groans, and eye rolls, because I certainly had a great time compiling this treasure trove of jokes for you.

Not only are these jokes for yourself to enjoy some laughs, but they are also for your family and friends. I have compiled these jokes with the intention of having your family and friends in stitches. While you may think most of them are not funny and really lame, that is what dad jokes are all about.

From one-liners to corny jokes, knock, knock jokes, short jokes, or long jokes, this book has it all. You have all the best jokes in one place, what more could a dad want? When you find yourself feeling bored, upset, or needing a laugh, pull this book out and open to any chapter for a good giggle and to feel lighter. Life is pretty serious as it is and all of us can use some laughter and lighthearted humor to take it easy.

I can speak from personal experience. As I had mentioned earlier, after my divorce with Mirabelle, our life was difficult. I honestly admit it was a depressing period in my life, one filled with changes, responsibilities, heartbreak, and sadness. It was not easy, but I pushed through, processing everything and finding humor in the places I could. I believe the humor really saved me from falling into a dark pit. Because I could find humor, even in the darkest times, I knew I could use it for my daughters to help them get through this change in their lives, and I did! I can confirm that it really helped. The days when we would sit around the dining table and everyone looked morose, I would pull out a joke or two and make them laugh. It just made the atmosphere lighter. I don't mean that all serious feelings and situations should be sidelined with humor, but heavier moments can be made lighter. I am a firm believer of talking about feelings, so please know that humor is not the answer to the problems. It is just a layer of light heartedness!

Even though my daughters wished and prayed Mirabelle and I would get back together, we couldn't, and at that point, humor, love, consideration, and care was all I could offer in return. Yes, I know, this joke book just took a serious turn! So back to the light-hearted side of life.

Before we end this hilarious journey, I want to give you some tips on how to land your jokes well. It's not just about the joke you are relating, there is much more involved. Remember the following rules:

1. If you are feeling awkward, try to relax because the other person will feed off your energy.
2. Keep your voice varied (this is important for longer jokes) because a monotone voice can get dull and boring.
3. Cue the punch line—pauses add excitement and suspense to joke telling.
4. Don't keep at the same joke.
5. Don't be desperate for a laugh; know when to exit the conversation gracefully.
6. Believe that the joke you are relating is actually very funny. When you believe in what you are saying, the other person will enjoy it more.
7. Use funny voices.
8. Enjoy yourself.

Moreover, I want to share a few lessons I have learned over the course of my life when it comes to jokes:

1. Older people don't appreciate poo and pee jokes.
2. Teens and younger adults enjoy mean and snarky jokes.
3. People who know about Socrates and Aristotle will appreciate Socrates and Aristotle jokes—nobody else will.
4. Laughing hysterically at your own joke after cracking it will not guarantee that the other person will laugh—unless your laugh is funnier than the joke.
5. Keep it simple.
6. Improvise and be spontaneous.
7. Watch standup comedians.
8. Don't offend others with humor. Know the difference between mean and funny.
9. Practice your jokes.
10. Observe other people you find funny.

I am sure all of us like to laugh from time to time, and I want to mix in dad jokes into this equation. Now, your audience's reaction is not in my hands and neither is laughter guaranteed. You could end up with eye rolls or laughter that brings a house down, but remember to have a good time!

This book has something for everyone, from your children to your family, friends, relatives, colleagues, and even yourself.

In this book I have covered jokes on the following topics

- the importance of humor
- animal antics
- making fun of the family
- food
- body references
- pop culture
- jobs and careers
- hobbies
- education
- fun times for the road
- STEM
- puns for teen children
- long story jokes
- the all-time best jokes

I've opened your eyes to an expansive world of jokes with this book! Don't forget the importance of humor and how it builds bonds, enhances connections, breaks the ice, and lightens tense situations. They are versatile and not just for situations where you want to make people laugh, it goes beyond that!

You can use all the jokes I have provided in the following situations:

- at home
- at your office
- at school
- with family
- with friends
- with colleagues
- in social gatherings

You get the point. You can basically use them anywhere! My daughters are now used to my humor and anticipate my jokes all the time. Sometimes, I feel my game is weakening, and I am going rusty. This is especially true when they say, "Dad, that was predictable." In those moments, I remind myself to up my game because hey, I don't want to be a predictable joker. I want the same for you; I don't want anyone to think *Oh no, not the same joke again*!

This book has fresh jokes, funny jokes, and never heard before jokes! I can assure you that nobody would have heard half of these jokes before. Now, it's time to decide which joke you want to crack on which victim! Go ahead and start choosing and get the laughs rolling.

I would highly appreciate it if you could leave a review on what you thought about this book. Your review will not only be important in helping you but also because we want to share the laughs with other dads and family members that need some fresh lines. Thank you and good luck.

REFERENCES

Definition of dad joke. (n.d.). https://www.merriam-webster.com/dictionary/dad+joke

Mitchell, H. (2019, February 27). What can science tell us about dad jokes? *Wall Street Journal.* https://www.wsj.com/articles/what-can-science-tell-us-about-dad-jokes-11551278885

Urban Dictionary: Yo momma jokes. (n.d.). Urban Dictionary. https://www.urbandictionary.com/define.php?term=yo%20momma%20jokes

What percentage of the average life of an american is spent at school? (2015, August 4). *Reference.Com.*

https://www.reference.com/world-view/percentage-average-life-american-spent-school-b4bf5e983cdb6f65

Why being funny is good for your family | parenting tips & advice. (n.d.). PBS KIDS for Parents. https://www.pbs.org/parents/thrive/why-being-funny-is-good-for-your-family

QUICK NOTE

Positive reviews from awesome customers like you help others to feel confident about choosing this book too. Would you take 60 seconds on Amazon or any platform where you got the book and share your happy experiences? There are other awesome books like *The First Time Father, The First Time Father: Baby's First Year, Sleep Training like a Pro, Single Dad Parenting Like a Pro, Potty Training Like a Pro, Discipline Like a Pro,* and *All Fathers Memorable Jokes* (others still to come.) Any topics you would like Alfie Thomas to write about, his email is always open. You can reach out to:

books@alfie-thomas.com and

https://thealfiethomas.com/

https://mirabellen.activehosted.com/f/1,

https://www.facebook.com/groups/1253933881690907, and

https://www.instagram.com/alfiethomas.official/

We will be forever grateful. Thank you in advance for helping us out.